The Vampire of the Continent

Graf E. Reventlow

(Translator: Georges Chatterton-Hill)

Alpha Editions

This edition published in 2024

ISBN : 9789362924186

Design and Setting By
Alpha Editions
www.alphaedis.com
Email - info@alphaedis.com

As per information held with us this book is in Public Domain.
This book is a reproduction of an important historical work. Alpha Editions uses the best technology to reproduce historical work in the same manner it was first published to preserve its original nature. Any marks or number seen are left intentionally to preserve its true form.

Contents

TRANSLATOR'S PREFACE .... - 1 -
CHAPTER I THE "HEROIC AGE" OF THE BRITONS SIXTEENTH CENTURY .... - 6 -
CHAPTER II THE PIOUS PIRATES SEVENTEENTH CENTURY .... - 13 -
CHAPTER III THE CAMPAIGN AGAINST THE "ENEMY OF PEACE" ERA OF LOUIS XIV .... - 20 -
CHAPTER IV "WE HAVE CONQUERED CANADA IN GERMANY" FREDERIC THE GREAT AND ENGLAND ...- 26 -
CHAPTER V THE PROTECTOR OF NEUTRAL COUNTRIES—THE LIBERATOR OF EUROPE SECOND HALF OF THE EIGHTEENTH CENTURY .... - 31 -
CHAPTER VI THE GREAT HARVEST THE NAPOLEONIC WARS .... - 44 -
CHAPTER VII ENGLAND DIGESTS HER BOOTY—THE CONTINENT GRADUALLY BECOMES UNRULY 1815–1890 .... - 55 -
CHAPTER VIII ANGLO-GERMAN FRIENDSHIP AND ESTRANGEMENT AFTER BISMARCK'S DEPARTURE 1890–1895 .... - 65 -
CHAPTER IX "AND IF THOU WILT NOT BE MY SERVANT...." FROM 1895 TILL THE ENTENTE CORDIALE .... - 70 -
CHAPTER X DELENDA GERMANIA THE BEGINNING OF KING EDWARD'S REIGN .... - 81 -
CHAPTER XI EDWARD VII PREPARES THE HUMILIATION AND DESTRUCTION OF GERMANY 1905–1908 .... - 83 -
CHAPTER XII THE INCENDIARY AT WORK THE CAMPAIGN AGAINST THE GERMAN NAVY .... - 89 -

CHAPTER XIII KING EDWARD'S UNSUCCESSFUL ATTEMPT TO SET THE NEAR EAST ABLAZE THE BOSNIAN CRISIS .... - 93 -

CHAPTER XIV THE CATASTROPHE IS MORE CAREFULLY PREPARED 1909–1914 .... - 102 -

TRANSLATOR'S PREFACE

Count Ernst zu Reventlow's book "The Vampire of the Continent," of which I have much pleasure in presenting a considerably abridged English edition to American readers, cannot be too strongly recommended to all those who desire to obtain an insight into the hidden recesses of European political history, where the forces are at work which have shaped the evolution of Europe since about the middle of the sixteenth century. It is the first systematic attempt to go to the root of things, to lay bare the developmental forces in question that have escaped the attention of partial or insufficiently clearsighted historians up till now. With rare penetration and skill does Count Reventlow show all such forces to find their synthesis in England's Will to Power—to use an expression coined by Nietzsche—in England's insatiable greed, in her limitless craving for the riches of this world. The center-point of European history during the last 350 years is to be found in London. It is here that have been spun all the threads of the countless political intrigues, the result of which has been to turn the palaces and cottages of Europe alike into shambles, her sunny fields and pastures into a desert deluged with human blood. And, meanwhile, the barns and granaries of England were filled with corn, her warehouses with goods of all descriptions from all corners of the globe; her factories and workshops poured forth their products with quadrupled energy; her warships prowled along the ocean highways, stealing all they could lay hands on, whether it belonged to friend or foe or neutral; and her trading vessels transported her manufactured articles to all countries, draining the wealth of the latter in exchange, and filling the pockets of the British merchant with gold.

The more greatly Europe was impoverished, the more did England's wealth increase. Therefore has England stirred up wars innumerable, in which she has herself taken practically no part, in order to ruin Europe economically, morally, and politically. Therefore has she always sought to prevent by all means the rise of any prosperous European State capable of competing with her in the markets of the world. She knew that, as long as she ruled the seas, Europe was helpless, and that the monopoly of the oversea trade belonged to her. Therefore did it become a fundamental principle of hers to destroy mercilessly the sea power of every nation, as soon as this sea power showed signs of growing to an extent such that England's "maritime supremacy" would be threatened.

Founded on piracy, the British Empire has been built up at the expense of humanity. The English commenced by robbing the Spanish treasure-ships—acts of murderous and dastardly brigandage which are held up to Englishmen to-day as deeds of prowess. They continued by robbing Canada and the

States from the French, Gibraltar from the Spaniards, India from the French and the Portuguese, South Africa from the Dutch, Egypt and Cyprus from the Turks, Malta from the Italians—and last, but not least, Ireland from the Irish. Over the whole world we can follow the trail of the venomous serpent, which has fastened its deadly fangs into so many victims. Over the whole world we hear the cry for vengeance and for redemption.

The great merit of Count Reventlow's work is that of showing us the history of Europe in its true light. Pitilessly has the historian here torn to shreds the garment of hypocrisy in which the English seek to clothe themselves; spurred on by the sole desire of impartiality searching for the truth, he has rent asunder the veil which they have thrown over the real history of the world with a cleverness equalled only by their unscrupulousness. England is here exposed to the reader in all her hideous nakedness, with not even a rag to cover her sores; in the cold, unshaded light of facts she appears before our eyes—no longer as the "Liberator," but as the Vampire saturated with the blood of its victims, as the Shylock gorged with ill-gotten wealth, as the Parasite grown fat on the marrow of the bones of all the peoples of the earth.

Count Reventlow's book is not only a book to be read; it should be re-read many times, pondered on, slowly and carefully digested; the great lessons it teaches us should be engraved in our minds. When the world has grasped the central truth taught by all the facts of its history during the last 350 years or thereabouts—the truth, namely, that Europe has never been considered by England as anything else but an instrument adapted to increasing the latter's wealth and power: then only can the salvation of the world be hoped for.

Spain, Holland, France, who, all of them, defended the interests of Europe against England, have been vanquished. But the victories of England were never obtained by England herself. Physical courage, endurance, organisation, are not characteristics of the Vampire. England's victories were obtained by Europe against Europe. From the outset England succeeded in trading on the ignorance and stupidity of Europe; admirably did she understand how to wave red cloths before the eyes of the European bulls, skilfully goaded to fury by her; equally admirably did she understand how to enthrall them with sententious phrases about "liberty" and "justice," even as the mermaids of old enthralled unsuspecting mariners by means of their divinely sweet melodies. The English Mermaid bewitched Europe with her Song of Liberty; and only too late has Europe discovered that it was a Song of Death.

But has she discovered it? We fear the truth is only just beginning to dawn. France at any rate does not yet perceive that she is being bled to death for the sake of England, who employs her to-day against Germany, even as she employed Germany against Louis XIV and Napoleon in former centuries.

France, Belgium, Russia, Italy, are to-day England's instruments. By means of them does she hope to destroy Germany and Austria-Hungary; but she also hopes that by destroying these, they will have eo ipso destroyed themselves. The whole of Europe will thus be drained to the last drop of blood, exhausted, ruined; and on those ruins will England's trade flourish anew. The harvest reaped as the result of the Napoleonic wars will be reaped again.

Such was England's calculation. It was a mistaken one. For the first time in her history since the Elizabethan period, England has miscalculated her chances. Grievously miscalculated them! Germany has to-day assumed the glorious task of liberating the world from the clutches of the British parasite. She it is who continues the great mission of Napoleon, who takes up the sword dropped by him, and which France, unfortunately, is to-day unwilling to wield. In this great war everyone must take his part—for it is a struggle between light and darkness, between truth and lies, between manly vigor and parasitical cowardice, between civilisation and barbarism. Germany, the champion of the light and the truth, against the power of darkness and mendacity! Under such circumstances, to sit on the fence would be contemptible. And those who cannot fight with the sword must fight with the pen.

Germany, in fighting for her own existence, is fighting also for the liberation of the world. The great day of liberation will surely come, sooner or later. The *conditio sine qua non* of that liberation is the destruction of England's maritime supremacy. For as long as England rules the waves, humanity must remain her slave. This is a fundamental truth. And another fundamental truth is that England's maritime supremacy cannot be destroyed until IRELAND IS A FREE COUNTRY.

The one criticism which can be levelled against Count Reventlow's admirable work is that it has not sufficiently insisted on this second great truth. As long as Ireland remains a British colony—or, rather, a British fortress—England can at any time shut off the whole of Northern and Eastern Europe from all access to the ocean; even as, by means of Gibraltar and Port Said and Aden, she can close the Mediterranean. Ireland is the key to the Atlantic. Release Ireland from her bondage, and the Atlantic is at once opened up to Europe.

Therefore must Ireland be restored to Europe, if Europe is to be free. An independent, neutral Irish Nation would be the natural bulwark of European liberty in the West. The freedom of Europe depends on the freedom of the seas; and the freedom of the seas depends on the liberation of Ireland.

We hear a lot about Ireland's helplessness and poverty. And it is nothing but trash accumulated by England's scribes and hirelings. Ireland, the most fertile country in Europe; Ireland, whose flourishing industry was deliberately destroyed by England; Ireland, whose civilisation reaches back far beyond the Christian Era into the dim twilight of the ages, and whose missionaries carried, during the early Middle Ages, the torch of learning and piety all over Western and Central Europe; Ireland, who, in the nineteenth century alone, whilst artificially-made famines wrought havoc amongst her children, furnished one thousand million pounds sterling to her oppressor for investment in the latter's world policy; Ireland, whose sturdy sons, broken on the wheel of misery, were decoyed to the number of 2,000,000 during the nineteenth century into England's army of mercenaries; Ireland, whose geographical position makes of her the connecting link between Europe and America, and whose forty harbors to-day lie empty and desolate at England's behest; Ireland, whose economic and biological wealth has formed the basis on which the whole structure of the British Pirate Empire has been reared:— Ireland is a rich country, rich by reason of her economic resources, and rich by reason of the incomparable moral qualities of the Irish race.

Europe has too long forgotten Ireland, too long has she shut her ears to Ireland's cry of distress. And to-day the most far-sighted of her thinkers and statesmen recognise that the secret of Europe's future destinies lies embedded in the green isle of Erin.

In his great speech in the Reichstag on August 19th, 1915, the German Chancellor, Herr von Bethmann-Hollweg, said: "The welfare of all peoples and nations demands that we obtain the freedom of the seas, not—as England has done—in order to rule the latter ourselves, but in order that they may serve equally the interests of all peoples." The words spoken by the Chancellor prove that Germany understands the nature of the immense historical task incumbent on her; and we may confidently believe that she likewise realises the conditions under which alone this task can be satisfactorily accomplished.

Despising the foul calumnies and the impotent vituperation of England's scribes, Erin waits calmly and confidently for the great day of her liberation. The best proofs of her invincible strength—proofs which no English lies can suppress—she carries within her bosom: namely, her Existence and her Faith. Alone against the most powerful empire in the world since the days of Rome, Ireland has survived. The British Butcher has tried in vain during three centuries to exterminate her; and yet, just before the war broke out, he was forced to hold out his gory hands in a vain attempt to coax the victim he had intended to strangle. Her race, her religion, her traditions, her language— Ireland has maintained them all, and yet no foreign help has been hers since the days of Napoleon. Often has she been deceived, but none the less is her faith to-day stronger than ever. For England's difficulty is Ireland's opportunity. These who, to-day, are intently listening, can hear the groan of an empire staggering under the blows rained mercilessly upon it—they can hear, as if borne on the wings of Time, a music like unto a distant death-knell, tolled by bells of the future cast by German hands, strong, swift, undaunted.

And meanwhile voices are calling to us, voices from the grave, the voices of our dead—of the martyrs who died for Ireland,—sacred voices that we hear both waking and in dreams, and that bid us watch and pray and be of good cheer, for the Green Flag of Erin is to-day unfurled in the whirlwind alongside of the Black, White, and Red.

G. C.-H.

Geneva, September MCMXV.

CHAPTER I
THE "HEROIC AGE" OF THE BRITONS
SIXTEENTH CENTURY

The average German considers the destruction of the Spanish Armada to have been a great and noble deed of liberation, for which the world owes an eternal debt of gratitude to England. This is what the German is taught at school, and this is what he reads in innumerable historical works. Spain, and above all the Spanish King Philip II, desired to force the whole of Europe into submission to the Catholic Church, and to prevent the development of the spirit of freedom. And behold! The Virgin Queen sends forth her fleet, and the world was saved: *afflavit Deus et dissipati sunt*. At the call of the Deity arose the mighty storm, which scattered the ships of the oppressor.

We may well ask the question as to when these epoch-making events will be revealed to the young German in another light? The naked reality of historical facts shows the matter to have had a very different aspect.

About the year 1500 Spain and Portugal were the two World-Powers. According to a decision of the Pope, the globe had been divided by a line of demarcation into two halves, of which the one belonged to Spain and the other to Portugal. Viewed in the light of those times, this somewhat naïve division of the globe was not an unjust one. The great discoveries of the preceding century had been made by Spain and Portugal, and they had opened out immense perspectives. Neither Power, however, grasped the fact that what was necessary to enable them to maintain their world-empires was not a mere Papal decree, but an ample armed force. They neglected their fleets; only too late did they perceive that in the North of Europe a nation had arisen, which instinctively recognised in piracy on the high seas the instrument adapted to its need of expansion. That nation was England.

Not a single Englishman is to be found among the pioneers who prepared the way for the great discoveries of the fifteenth and sixteenth centuries. Neither do we find among the English any record of journeys like those accomplished by the Vikings of old—journeys undertaken for the sole pleasure of adventure, and of exploring unknown and distant regions. We find, on the other hand, alike in the English nation and in its rulers, an extremely shrewd comprehension of the value of gold and silver—a comprehension already highly developed at that period. The news of the incredible wealth derived by Spain and Portugal from those oversea possessions which the genius of their citizens had permitted them to discover, gave the English chronic insomnia. They had themselves neither discovered nor taken possession of anything. What, therefore, more natural for them than the idea of stealing from others what these others possessed?

The idea was, indeed, the more natural, seeing that Spain and Portugal had neglected to build up their fleet. Thus began, as British historians solemnly tell us, the "heroic age" of the English people. It was an age characterised by organised piracy and highway robbery; which was at first tolerated, and subsequently sanctioned, by the English sovereigns—especially by the Virgin Queen, the champion of Protestantism.

English piracy sailed under the flag of Protestantism, and of the liberation from Rome. Leaders such as Hawkins, Frobisher, and Sir Francis Drake fitted out expeditionary fleets and sailed over the ocean to the Spanish and Portuguese possessions in America. But their favorite trick was to lie in waiting for the Spanish ships filled with gold and silver, which they captured and brought in triumph to England, where these pirates were welcomed by Queen and people as champions of the Protestant faith, no less than of civilisation and progress. Or else they sailed to Spain herself,—without ever war having been declared,—and flung themselves like a pack of hungry wolves on the vessels at their moorings in Cadiz or Vigo, which they promptly robbed, burnt, and sank; they then destroyed docks and warehouses, and massacred everyone they could find. This went on for years. But woe betide any "naval commander" who dared to return home without a rich booty in gold, silver, or colonial produce! Even if his life was spared, he could be sure of a long term of imprisonment, and of the lasting dislike of the Queen. In return for their heroic efforts on behalf of religious freedom, the English wished to have at least plenty of ships filled with gold and silver.

Spain at last resolved to put an end to English piracy, and the Armada was built. The English did not succeed in preventing the construction of the Spanish fleet by their attacks on Spanish ports, and by burning docks and vessels at anchorage therein—albeit Drake destroyed 150 ships and an immense quantity of provisions in Cadiz in 1587. The following year Philip of Spain endeavored, by means of the Armada, to punish the English pirate nation, and to ensure once for all the safety of Spanish property. The unsuccessful result of the expedition is well known; we would only recall the fact that the Duke of Parma was waiting with an army in the Spanish Netherlands, and that a fleet was at his disposal in order to permit of his rejoining the Armada, and of landing in Great Britain. England did not adopt the only attitude suitable for her, namely that of the ambushed highway robber—but adopted instead the attitude of a defender of the Protestant faith. We still read to-day, in English history books, that Philip of Spain fitted out the Armada in order to force the doctrines of Catholicism down the throats of the English. The good Continental Protestants were full of admiration for the sacrifices endured by England in order to prevent a disaster to the pure doctrine.

All the fundamental principles of Great Britain's insular policy were manifested during the long years of war between England and Spain—war which resulted finally in the destruction of the Armada, and the complete upsetting of the plan to invade England by way of the Netherlands. British policy, from the earliest times of British expansion, has always remained the same, even if (according to Clausewitz) it has subsequently adopted different means for attaining its ends.

When English sailors, under the protection of the Queen or on her suggestion, systematically pounced upon Spanish property; when they attacked, in time of peace, the Spanish coasts, or Spanish ships on the high seas, or Spanish oversea possessions, there was never any sort of question of British rights, or of legitimate British interests, or of the defence of British homes, or of the protection of the Protestant faith. The English simply coveted that which others possessed; and they were angry that others had it, and not themselves. Above all things they wanted gold. Not only the ancient English historians, but also the modern ones, admit this as something which is self-evident. Whenever an English "naval commander" cruised during months, or even years, on the high seas, in order to capture a fleet of Spanish galleys carrying gold and silver; when, in the midst of peace, he undertook a marauding expedition against Spanish or Portuguese ports, in order to rob, burn, and massacre to his heart's content, he was received on his return as a hero of the Protestant faith—provided he had been successful. If he came home with empty hands, he was despised. The "treasure-ships," i. e. galleys laden with gold and silver, play an extraordinary part, which the German reader can at first hardly understand, in the descriptions of that "heroic age." But the ambitions of the English heroes of the faith were not limited to the ships alone; with the sure instinct of the bandit *de grand style*, they soared beyond them, as far as the countries from which the precious metal came. Drake's "voyage around the world," which is still admired in Germany as the deed of prowess of an idealistic pioneer of civilisation, was nothing else than a thieves' raid. Admiral Freemantle wrote a few years ago concerning it: "Drake undertook an extensive cruise, in the course of which he burnt and plundered the wealthy coast towns of the Spanish colonies, beginning with Valparaiso, the capital of Chili. He continued his journey, seizing all the treasures he could lay hands on.... He returned to Plymouth in triumph, the first Englishman who had sailed round the world, and laden with a million of pounds' worth of booty. Honored by his Queen, beloved of his countrymen, he then put to sea once more, in order, as he expressed it, to singe the King of Spain's beard. This time he left England, not as a private adventurer, but as an English Admiral, backed up by the authority of the Queen."

Drake embodied the English ideal of heroism, and still embodies it to-day. The form alone under which that ideal incorporates itself has altered, although even the alteration of form is less great than is generally supposed.

Throughout English history, and up till the present day, we can trace the constant application of three methods: firstly, destruction of the means which the nation whom it is intended to rob possesses for protecting its property on the seas and oversea—i. e. its fleet, harbors, docks, etc.; secondly, the seizure or destruction of the trading vessels of such a nation. When these aims have been realised, England lays hands without further difficulty on that nation's oversea possessions. It is to be observed, that this policy and this method of warfare depend in the last instance for their success on the weakening of England's continental rivals. When the sea power of the latter has been broken, the colonies fall off automatically, so to speak.

For the first time in English history we now see, during the Elizabethan period, the relations between England, on the one hand, and the Netherlands and Belgium, on the other, clearly delineated. The Netherlands, as we know, formerly included Holland and Belgium, and belonged entirely to Spain till 1579; after this date Holland became independent, while Belgium remained in Spanish hands. From the beginning, England viewed the Spanish Netherlands as a dangerous outpost of the Spanish world-empire. She did everything she could to assist the Netherlands in their struggle for liberty, and to detach them from Spain. The London Government hoped, in this case, to have a weak state at the other side of the Channel and the North Sea—a state naturally inclined to be serviceable to England. The planned invasion of the latter by a Spanish army stationed in Holland, has become, for British statesmen, a never-to-be-forgotten nightmare. From that day on the decision was taken, never to allow Belgium and Holland to come under the influence of any Power save England. As soon as the sea power of Spain had been broken, England's interest was absorbed by a new problem: how to prevent the Netherlands from becoming themselves a strong Sea Power.

If England came to the help of the Netherlands in their struggle against Spain, she did so, of course, under the pretext of defending the cause of Protestantism. The real reason, however, was to prevent any nation with sea power behind it from obtaining property and influence at the other side of the Channel. It is very conceivable that the English statesmen of those days did not first enunciate this principle as a theory, and put it subsequently into practice. On the contrary, they invariably acted in accordance with the requirements of practical necessity. Neither must the experiences be forgotten, that England had made in the course of many centuries during which her ambition had been to become a Continental Power. She had tried hard to obtain rights of property on the French coast, and in the whole of France. If England finally abandoned her efforts in this direction, it was because she recognised that her insular position, in regard to European nations, far from being a weak one, was very strong. As a consequence of this recognition, arose her growing dislike to the despatch of English troops to the Continent. Her fighting forces must be kept in the country, so as not to sacrifice them except on very favorable occasions. The destruction of the Spanish Armada entailed the recognition of another great truth: namely, that an invasion of England was not to be feared, as long as the English fleet retained the mastery of the sea. A corollary of this truth was, that every continental fleet must be considered to be a potential enemy of England's prosperity and safety; and, further, that the danger must be considered to increase in proportion as the harbors serving as a basis for such a fleet are near to the English coasts.

In this way did English statesmen come to the decision to employ on the Continent, as far as possible, foreign soldiers to fight England's battles; for the native troops, as we have said, must be kept in the country. The only possibility of applying such a decision in practical life, lay in inducing the Continental Powers to let their armies fight for England's interests. In order to carry out this policy it was indispensable that the Powers in question should be made to believe that, in combating England's enemies, they were at the same time defending their own interests, if not their own existence. Henceforth were the main lines to be followed by English policy in its dealings with the Continent, definitely laid down. The means adopted for pursuing that policy were made to depend entirely on two factors: the circumstances of the moment, and the adversary to be dealt with. From the very outset it was tacitly admitted that nothing could be so disadvantageous for the realisation of English aims, than harmony among the Continental States, i. e. peace in Europe. Peace must inevitably bring about increased prosperity; and the consequence will be the growth of the sea power of Continental nations, alike in the waters in the neighborhood of England, and on the ocean. Sea power is the typical expression of the inner strength and unity of a nation—of a strength which must expand abroad because it cannot find adequate employment within the limits of the mother country. But it was precisely this growing prosperity of the European Continent of which England had no need!

Very early did the English Kings come to understand the value of industry for a country. As the English mind was not productive in this domain, skilled workers were, in the later Middle Ages, systematically recruited abroad. The manufacture of cloth, weaving, mining, ironwork, machinery, dyeing—all these industrial arts were brought to England by German, Dutch and French artisans. In this way was the incapacity of the English people compensated for. The narrowness of mind, quarrelsomeness, and intolerance of the Germans proved very useful in this respect; all the dissatisfied or persecuted

German artisans went over to England. The stream of emigrants grew constantly larger as a result of the wars of religion. The English industry was slowly developed behind the impregnable wall of a prohibitively high tariff. As long as trade and industry and art were able to flourish in Germany, England was wholly unable to compete with them; for the German products were immeasurably superior to the English ones. But when the Empire decayed in strength as a consequence of political and religious dissensions, industrial and commercial regression likewise set in; and England did everything she could to hasten the downfall. Whilst England was undertaking, during the sixteenth century, the freebooters' war against Spain of which we have already spoken; whilst she was thereby increasing her sea power to such an extent as to become, at times, the mistress of the ocean;—during this time the power of the German Hansa was broken, and the last emblem of the latter's former greatness, the Hanseatic Steel Court in London, disappeared in the last years of the sixteenth century.

During one hundred and fifty years English ships continued to carry out the policy of burning, murdering, and stealing immense treasures which were taken off to England; all this was done in the name of religion, and more particularly of Protestant freedom. The Germans, meanwhile, were busy slaughtering each other, and dissolving their empire in religious strife; the Thirty Years' War turned the once prosperous country into a desert, and annihilated the whole of that flourishing industry which had been the admiration of the world. England fanned to the utmost possible extent the flames of German religious strife. The English were pious people—especially the English Kings and Queens; they were of opinion that the Germans were perfectly justified in transforming their own country into a cesspool of human blood, for the glory of God and of the Protestant faith. In this manner was England spared the disagreeable necessity of fighting a dangerous competitor. The German wars of religion, the hopeless want of unity among the Germans, were among the important factors that contributed to the establishment, in later times, of the English monopoly of trade and industry. The stolen gold of Spain and Portugal, on the other hand, constituted the basis on which the future edifice of English capitalism was reared. English capital, in turn, admitted of goods being manufactured and delivered cheaply; and this cheapness rendered subsequently all competition with British industry impossible. Soon the home market was not sufficient, and English goods were brought to other lands under the protection of the English fleet, mistress of the seas.

At the end of the sixteenth century the East India Company was founded. Twenty years later England stole from the Portuguese the important commercial center of Ormuz, in the Persian Gulf. An English historian remarks drily that "this action marks the beginning of our supremacy in those waters." The same historian writes: "An attempt was made to obtain possession of the Spanish colonies in Germany and Holland by means of a sudden raid. The enterprise failed owing to the unskilful leadership of the Earl of Mansfield. After this failure, the English Court applied all its resources to the fitting out of a fleet, in order that Cadiz might be sacked, and the Spanish treasure-ships captured." Great was the grief and anger in England when the unsuccessful raiders came back empty-handed from their excursion to Holland.

In the course of her "heroic age," England laid the foundations of her future supremacy; she did so by means of brigandage and theft, of violence and treachery, after she had perceived the strength of her insular position and had learnt how to utilise that strength. Her rulers had recognised the value of a national industry, and had understood the means best calculated to favor its growth.

The English of those days were by no means supermen. They were not more intelligent than other nations; on the contrary, during the era of discoveries they discovered nothing, and during the era of inventions they invented nothing. But they understood the art of ploughing their fields by means of stolen oxen. And that which very clearly distinguished them from every other European people was the greed of lucre as the fundamental mainspring of action.

CHAPTER II
THE PIOUS PIRATES
SEVENTEENTH CENTURY

Whereas the whole of the once prosperous German industry disappeared in the course of the Thirty Years' War, leaving a convenient vacancy for English production to fill; this was by no means the case with the Netherlands. After the separation of the latter from Spain, their industry and commerce reached an unprecedented height of development. Colonies were acquired in East India, in the Indian Ocean, in North America, and in South Africa. During the German wars of religion, the Netherlands offered a place of refuge to many of the best elements of the German population, and also convenient and profitable investments for their money. Emigrants and investments contributed very largely to the growing prosperity of the little country. If the German Empire had evolved normally, Holland would have become its "window" opening on to the North Sea and the Channel. Nature would certainly seem to have destined the Netherlands, including Belgium, to play this part. But the German Empire had been turned into a desert, and its commercial importance had ceased to exist.

The fact that Holland was able to become, in the seventeenth century, the greatest Sea Power in Europe, is all the more remarkable in view of the circumstances. And inevitably the question arises: what would have happened if only the Netherlands could have been amalgamated with the German Empire, as Nature intended them to be?

The Netherlands were everywhere in England's way: whether as maritime Power or commercial Power, in European or in British waters, on the high seas or in the colonies. This could not be tolerated. Least of all could the Dutch be forgiven for having acquired rights of property there where the English had so far only claims—in North America and India, and especially on the high road between India and China. England saw at once that she must have recourse to those weapons which had already proved so successful in the case of Spain and Portugal: the roots of Dutch sea power must be cut off, so that the fruit might then fall without further effort into the hands waiting to gather it. Unfortunately the majority of the Dutch were not Catholics, so that the war of destruction against their commerce could not conveniently be carried on under the pretence of defending the Protestant faith. England understood this, and chose another pretext accordingly.

Puritanism was now dominant in England. The pious regicide Cromwell had uttered the significant words: "Pray and keep your powder dry." It is certain that the carrying out of this last recommendation entailed considerably more work than did the praying! The Germans have been in the habit of searching in English Puritanism for ideals which it never contained. The mainspring of Puritanism was the fanatical belief that the English people constitutes a divinely chosen race, which is destined to reign over all other nations and to monopolise the world's commerce. The "religious enthusiasm" of which it boasted did, in the long run, but serve the ends of egotism. As a matter of fact, Puritanism never got beyond the Ego; and it was fundamentally irreligious. It believed itself to be entrusted with the mission of founding the Kingdom of God on earth. But this Kingdom of God was nothing if not a world-empire dominated by England; and its realisation further implied that the Chosen People of God should have the entire trade of humanity exclusively in their hands. Here we have the real spirit of Puritanism; and it is neither an exaggeration nor a misrepresentation to describe it as we have done. The pharisaical creed of a greedy and thieving race which, living in the security of an island fortress, cast, like unto a pack of vultures, its lustful glances over seas and continents—this hypocritical creed could not possibly recognise the Protestantism of other nations to be anything like as pure as that of its own adherents. A Christian people which should be stupid and criminal enough not to grovel in the dust before the Chosen Nation—which should even push such criminal folly to the extent of competing with that Chosen Nation on the sea: such a people deserves nothing else but annihilation. The God of the English commands it!

It was not a mere accident that precisely those pious men should have waxed ever more indignant at the spectacle of Holland's prosperity, who were always ready to commit every crime calculated to ensure the glory of God and of England. Their indignation was justified; during the first half of the seventeenth century, at the very moment when a certain reaction was visible in England after the "heroic age," Holland had risen to the first rank alike as a trading Power, a maritime Power, and a colonial Power. By means of indomitable energy the Dutch had succeeded, if not in monopolising the oversea trade, at least in acquiring the lion's share of it. Their trading ships sailed along every coast, and did a very considerable carrying trade to and from English ports. Dutch industry flourished, and proved a serious competitor for English manufacturers on the Continental markets. The Chosen People on the other side of the Channel could not possibly tolerate such a state of affairs. The Puritan Cooper proclaimed that *"delenda est Carthago."* Carthage must be destroyed, Protestant Holland must be crushed, for she is in our way!

This was Cromwell's view. In 1651 he caused the celebrated Navigation Act to be passed. Henceforth it was forbidden to carry foreign freights to English ports on other than English ships, or else ships belonging to the nation exporting the freights in question. It was a death-blow dealt at Holland's carrying trade. England likewise required all foreign ships to salute in future the English flag whenever they should meet it. The Chosen People thus demanded that all other seafaring nations should recognise its claim to rule the seas—and this was 250 years ago! But this was not all. Cromwell demanded further for English warships in war time the right of searching all trading vessels belonging to neutral nations, in order to see whether or not the latter had goods on board which belonged to the enemy. We have already said that the Dutch ships were very numerous, and that they often had very valuable freight on board; as one may imagine, it was a splendid opportunity for the pious and morally pure English pirates to satisfy their greed under the pretext of the "right of search." Innumerable neutral vessels were captured, brought to English harbors, there to await the decisions of the English Prize Courts. The latter had already in the seventeenth century—just like they have in 1915—the inestimable advantage of always condemning a captured ship, provided the latter and its freight be of some value. The Dutch declined to submit to the convenient English custom. This angered the English so much, that Cromwell gave orders to Admiral Black suddenly to attack the Dutch fleet in the midst of peace, under the pretext that the Dutch Admiral Van Tromp had refused to salute the English flag. Thus began the great war between Holland and England, which lasted, with interruptions, until 1674.

If that war had taken place in our days, Dutch statesmen would probably have said, on the eve of its outbreak: "Not a single question can arise between Holland and England, capable of causing a war between two civilised nations who are also bound to each other by links of blood." A crowd of people unable to form a judgment of their own would have accepted such cheap wisdom with enthusiasm, and would have abundantly denounced all those who held different opinions as jingoes, super-patriots, and so forth. It is all the more important for us, in judging the part played by England in the present war, that we should understand how Elizabethan England waged war on sea, simply because jealous of other people's prosperity; and how Cromwellian England, and the England of later times, waged wars under different forms, but with the same underlying purpose. Englishmen and Anglophile Germans have called the war of destruction carried on by England against Holland a "commercial war"—thinking thereby to justify it. Let us for a moment examine the question as to what a so-called "commercial war" means. By dint of hard work, enterprise, and skill, a nation has acquired a high position as a commercial and maritime Power. Another nation, less clever and less capable, becomes filled with jealousy at the sight, and declares: "It is contrary to our dignity and to God's commandments, therefore must the criminal be destroyed." About twenty-five years ago an English review, alarmed by the first signs of a development of German trade, wrote: "If Germany were extinguished to-morrow, the day after to-morrow there is not an Englishman in the world who would not be the richer. Nations have fought for years over a city or a right of succession; must they not fight for two hundred and fifty million pounds of yearly commerce?" At the time there were many, in Germany, who were of opinion that no importance was to be attached to such utterances as this, seeing that the England of modern times is a civilised Power loving peace. It is to be presumed that these simple minds have learnt something in the meantime!

It would be a pity not to mention, while we are about it, a significant passage which we found in the work of a British naval officer some half-dozen years ago. (The work in question had obtained a prize.) "We—i. e. England—do not go to war for sentimental reasons. I doubt if we ever did. War is the outcome of commercial quarrels; it has for its aims the forcing of commercial conditions by the sword on our antagonists, conditions which we consider necessary to commercially benefit us. We give all sorts of reasons for war, but at the bottom of them all is commerce. Whether the reason given be the retention or obtaining of a strategical position, the breaking of treaties, or what not, they come down to the bed-rock of commerce, for the simple and effective reason that commerce is our life-blood."

The above quotation should be inserted as a preface to every history of England, and to every discussion of English politics. The passages reproduced here are in truth classical by reason of their brevity and clearness; and they were not written by some obscure scribbler, but by a British naval officer to whom a prize was awarded for his work by a committee composed of politicians, economists, and naval men.

England assisted Holland in the latter's struggle against Spain, under the pretext of serving the cause of Protestant freedom. During the war of destruction subsequently waged by her against Protestant Holland, England relied for help on Catholic France. While England had, in the sixteenth century, given herself out as the "champion of political freedom," and had in this capacity come to the help of the Netherlands, she allied herself, in the seventeenth century, just as enthusiastically with the absolutist French monarchy, in order to destroy republican Holland.

During the war with Holland, the typical insular policy of England assumed definite shape. This policy consists in regarding the European Continent exclusively as a means to an end; and in taking sides for or against a Power, or group of Powers, according as English interests shall dictate it. It may be objected that English interests do not necessarily remain identical in each succeeding century; and that the point of view from which they must be judged will consequently differ. But to this, we may reply: English interests have always remained the same throughout the centuries, and their basis has invariably been a commercial one. And experience, which every century in succession has confirmed, shows that English commerce develops, and that England grows ever richer, in the measure that the Continent is impoverished. The impoverishment of the Continent, in turn, grew in the measure that the nations inhabiting it were divided among themselves. With regard to the war between England and Holland, it must be observed that the latter had never aspired towards territorial expansion, and had never been one of the great European Powers. England could not even allege, as a pretext for the war, that Holland had disturbed the peace of the Continent, and must therefore be destroyed in the interests of that peace. None the less did England proclaim: *Carthaginem esse delendam.*

We must not overlook the immense historical importance of the fact that the two first wars of robbery and destruction waged by England were directed against Spain and Holland: against the former, on account of her position at the junction of the Atlantic and the Mediterranean; against the latter, on account of her position on the shores of the North Sea and the Channel. Both these parts of the European Continent have ever since had the greatest strategical and commercial importance for England.

The first step towards the establishment of British supremacy in the Mediterranean was taken by Admiral Blake in the middle of the seventeenth century. Alleged acts of piracy committed on the coasts of Tunis, Algeria, and Tripoli furnished the necessary motive. Blake came to an agreement with the Bey of Tunis, to the effect that no English ship should in future be held up. The ships of other nations were left out of consideration as being without any importance. This event is in itself insignificant, yet it marks the opening of a new epoch in history. From that time onwards has England's supremacy in the Mediterranean, although neither recognised nor absolute, none the less been a problem of worldwide interest. The same Admiral Blake then went with his fleet into the Atlantic, where he joined Admiral Montagu's squadron, and waited for the Spanish treasure-ships from South America and the West Indies. They soon captured rich booty, with which Montagu returned home. But Blake waited for the rest of the Spanish treasure-ships till the spring of 1657. After more than two years, as English historians boastfully tell us, his patience was rewarded, and he attacked the treasure-ships in the harbor of Teneriffe. The Spaniards—who were criminal enough to defend their property—were massacred, their ships and port destroyed. We have recounted this little episode, because it shows us so clearly how the pious and puritan English, with their eyes lifted up to Heaven, prepared the way for the Kingdom of God on earth.

In the middle of her war against Holland, the opportunity presented itself for England to temporarily make peace with her adversary; whereupon she promptly concluded an alliance with Holland and Sweden against Louis XIV. of France. We likewise only mention this little episode in order to furnish a fresh proof of the ease with which England has always changed her alliances and her enemies according as the occasion required it. In order to facilitate such changes, it is customary to periodically shift the men in power. Four years after the feat accomplished by Blake, an English squadron under Admiral Holmes attacked a large Dutch trading fleet coming from the Levant, at the moment when it was entering the Channel. English arrogance has, be it observed, long since added to the word "Channel" the prefix "English." Holmes' exploit served as introduction to the last and decisive period of the war. England and France were united. In 1674 Holland recognised, by the Treaty of Westminster, the British supremacy on the seas. England's rival had disappeared from the scene.

Henceforth Holland became England's ally and protégé; the English nation and its rulers guarded henceforth jealously the "liberty" of the Dutch, and showed themselves to be passionate defenders of the rights of the weak, of the sacredness of treaties, and of the balance of power. In the course of time the balance of power has not only become a dogma of British policy; but it has become a practical criterion, according to which this policy has been systematically applied in every concrete case. England is in the habit of addressing the world in the following terms: "Our policy aims at securing a balance of power on the Continent, in order that peace may reign there, and that no European State may develop at the expense of another." In the course of many centuries of struggle for justice and liberty, Great Britain has acquired the privilege of styling herself the legitimate protectress of these ideals, common to the whole of humanity. Such is the English contention! In reality the English policy of the balance of power means simply the stirring up of as many European Powers as possible against the nation which Great Britain, at any given time, considers as her most dangerous competitor. This nation is, of course, always the one which, thanks to its strength and prosperity, threatens to destroy the commercial monopoly of the Chosen People.

As a result of the war with Holland, after which the two countries were bound by dynastic links, and as a result, likewise, of the further dynastic connection with Hanover, England established herself once more on the Continent. The circumstances were far more favorable for her now than in previous centuries, when she endeavored to conquer France by force of arms. The new method was cheaper and less risky. Holland and Hanover became the outposts of Great Britain in Europe; a part of the coasts of the North Sea and the Channel became de facto British. Such outposts possessed vast importance for England's continental trade, and were also admirable political trump-cards. As for the participation of England in the continental wars, it was a fundamental principle of British policy not to allow the precious blood of Albion's sons to be shed. But the British Government was consequently all the more generous with the blood of its continental mercenaries. The latter were allowed the honor of having their bones broken for the English idea of the balance of power in Europe. It is evident that the influence on European politics alike of the English dynasty and of the English Government, was immensely increased by these new continental connections.

A large part of the Spanish and Dutch colonies fell into English hands, and the maritime power of Holland was broken during the long war, during which Dutch trading vessels were captured and destroyed *en masse*. The neutral countries were obliged to submit to their ships being held up and searched by English cruisers, during every war which it pleased the English Government to wage. Such neutral ships generally disappeared then for good into English harbors. As soon as the Prize Court, with its usual solemnity and impartiality, had pronounced a ship and its freight to be lawful booty, both were promptly transferred into English hands, and the English trading fleet was increased by so much.

This method proved most lucrative. Its steady application paved the way for England's future trade monopoly. Foreign flags disappeared progressively from the high seas, and were replaced by English ones. In this simple manner did England obtain possession of the thriving Dutch trade in the Far East.

CHAPTER III
THE CAMPAIGN AGAINST THE "ENEMY OF PEACE" ERA OF LOUIS XIV

England now turned her attention to the third European Power, whose expansion and prosperity caused ever-growing anxiety to the Chosen People: namely France. Under her Kings the latter country had developed into a homogeneous, centralised state. By means of a clever and unscrupulous foreign policy, in conjunction with the energy of an essentially progressive population, France had been able to profit immensely by the weakness and lack of unity of the German Empire. The German wars of religion, and especially the Thirty Years' War, afforded France the most magnificent opportunities for expansion. By far the strongest European Power, France was also a maritime and colonial Power of the first rank. The great statesman Colbert succeeded, by his wise and far-sighted administration, in raising trade and industry to an unprecedented height of prosperity. A bold and skilful colonial policy was pursued in India, North and South America. In Canada and in the southern States of the Union, the travels of intrepid French explorers had opened up for their country immense regions, the possession of which made France the foremost nation in America, even as she was the foremost in the East Indies. Recognised as the leading European Power, France was in a fair way to becoming the leading World-Power. Her strength, and consequently the validity of her claims, resided in the fact of her possessing this pre-eminent continental situation, as also in the facts of her political homogeneity and of the wonderful productivity of her inhabitants. During the second half of the seventeenth century, the people of England became aware of the existence of a dangerous rival; and an English historian tells us that the learned men at his side of the Channel at once enunciated the theory of Louis XIV being the enemy of European peace and consequently of England. For the moment, however, political circumstances in England did not permit of the latter carrying out her designs. She needed the "enemy of peace" to help her first of all in her war of robbery and destruction against Holland. Louis XIV, allied with England, waged war against the Dutch on land and sea. His chief desire was to destroy the Dutch trade; but when peace had been concluded between Holland and England, and Louis XIV found himself alone at war with the Dutch, the whole of the carrying trade, which the French had succeeded in wresting from the former, passed necessarily into the hands of neutral England. The war brought no advantage to French trade, and Louis recognised too late that he had labored solely for England. Not only had this labor been in vain, as far as France was concerned; but the maritime trade of the latter country was, as a consequence of the war, taken over to a large extent by Albion's merchants.

Nature had destined France to be a maritime and commercial Power of the highest rank. She has three magnificent coasts. Her geographical position seemed to make her the heir of Spain—and not only the heir, but also the conqueror, in which case she must have extended her dominions as far as the Pillars of Hercules. It was inevitable that France should, in the North, turn her eyes towards the Spanish Netherlands (i. e. Belgium), and, further still, towards Holland. In this way, the two countries at the expense of which England had risen to power, appeared destined to become simple dependencies of France. The War of the Spanish Succession arose about the question of the future relations between Paris and Madrid. Louis XIV claimed the Spanish throne for his grandson, after the death of its actual occupant. Had this claim been successful, France would not only have seen her continental power immensely increased by the possession of the entire sea-coast from Dunkerque to Gibraltar, and from Gibraltar to Toulon—but all the Spanish colonies would have been henceforth incorporated in the already large French colonial empire. Last, but not least, France would have taken over the whole of the trade with these new colonies. The last-mentioned point was precisely the most important of all. At that time, every colonial Power claimed for itself the right of a monopoly of trade with its colonies. Spain and Portugal still possessed, despite all that had been stolen from them by England, large and wealthy colonies. Had these been annexed to the French colonial empire, an essentially French character would have been given to the whole of the oversea colonial world.

The English art of inducing Continental nations to fight Albion's battles manifested itself in its perfection during the Anglo-French wars at the end of the seventeenth and the beginning of the eighteenth century. The Netherlands, Prussia, and especially Austria, were stirred up against France, and nothing was left undone in order to involve the latter in ever fresh wars. England's statesmen knew perfectly well, already at that epoch, that such wars weaken all the Continental Powers, that they increase their national debt, paralyse their trade and industry, and render them impotent on the seas. A few years ago an English Imperialist, Sir Harold Wyatt, wrote that naval wars are always a time of harvest for England. The latter had already learnt this lesson from her Dutch war. Admiral Freemantle and other English historians speak with pride of the era when the English fleet began to undertake the duties of "policeman of the seas," and to impose the *pax britannica* on all by force. The right of policing the seas has since been considered a Divine right of the Chosen People. This right consists in stealing as many trading vessels, whether neutral or not, as possible, under some pious and lying pretext.

Especially did the English need Austria, the old adversary of France— Austria, who had been ousted by France from her position as foremost

European Power. In the seventeenth century Austria had a particularly heavy burden to bear: the wars with the Turks. These wars were very welcome to England, as long as they seemed to endanger Austria's existence. In the same way as England manifested a deeply sympathetic interest in the welfare of Christianity and human progress, so did she consider the advance of the Turks through the Balkan Peninsula and the plains of Hungary with the unruffled calm of the businessman, who knows in advance the profit he will reap. The late Alexander von Peez, one of those who knew best the motives underlying English mercantile policy, wrote: "The Duke of Argyle tells us that in 1683, when the Turks attempted to take Vienna by storm, the sympathy of the Whigs was with the Turks. The trading classes, whose political representatives the Whigs were, wished and hoped to see Vienna captured by the Mussulmans." The reasons for such a pious hope were evident: a victory of the Turks would have produced incalculable effects in the whole of South-Eastern Europe. The triumph of the Crescent would have spelt the destruction, or at any rate the prolonged paralysis, of industry and commerce in all the Austrian lands. In itself this implied an immense advantage for the English business world; for the latter would then have been, in all those regions occupied by the Turks, without any competition, and it could consequently have fixed the prices to suit its convenience. The German wars of religion, and the persecution of the French Protestants, had taught the English that, under circumstances such as would necessarily have prevailed in the countries conquered by the Turks, the capitalists tend to emigrate and to seek refuge in England; whereby the capital invested in the latter naturally increases.

The Austrians were disobliging enough to offer a successful resistance. English diplomacy then set itself to induce the Emperor Leopold to stem himself the tide of his troops' victory, and to send his triumphant armies away to the west of Europe. An English journal of that period expressed itself, according to Peez, as follows: "Emperor Leopold, having placed the general interest of Europe (England?) above his own, has withdrawn a large part of his troops from Hungary and the Lower Danube, and transferred them to the Rhine; as a result, Belgrade and Nish have been re-taken by the Turks." When we consider these matters with calm impartiality, we are always tempted to ask ourselves: which was the most remarkable, the cleverness of England or the stupidity of the others? We believe the last of these two factors to have been the most important, and Austrians will probably share this opinion to-day. England did not desire to see Austria-Hungary develop into a Balkan Power; the former has always regarded every expansion of other nations—especially when seacoasts, harbors, navigable streams, come into play—as an insult to the Chosen People and a menace to European peace. Thus did Austria voluntarily sacrifice the fruits of her victory, in order to place herself in England's service against France. Germany furnished, according to an ancient and hallowed custom, the battlefields. The only Power which reaped any profits was, of course, England. Had it not been for the Franco-Austrian quarrels, William of Orange would never have ascended the English throne. Very rightly has Peez said: "England's freedom was saved by long wars on the Rhine, by the devastation of the Palatinate, by the sacrificing of the fruits of Austrian victories in the South-East."

For our own part we always bear in mind the imprudent words of Disraeli: "England's influence has never been stronger than when her motives have not been suspected." Whenever her interests—or, as we should prefer to say, her greed—demanded that a Continental State should be destroyed or weakened, the London Cabinet always knew how to create complications for that State, and it then came to the support of the latter's enemies by one means or another. The countries to whose help she came were, of course, very grateful, and England's virtues were celebrated with enthusiasm. She was reputed a free country, which espoused, solely for moral reasons, the cause of religious liberty against tyranny and intolerance. Only much later did the Continental nations begin to see that the whole thing was purely and simply a matter of business, and extremely lucrative business, for Albion. And some nations have not understood it even now!

The War of the Spanish Succession likewise brought in a rich harvest for England. When the Peace of Utrecht was concluded in 1713, England was the only maritime Power in the world. The late well-known American historian, Admiral Mahan, describes England's position at that period as follows: "England ... meanwhile was building up a navy, strengthening, extending and protecting her commerce, seizing maritime positions,—in a word, founding and rearing her sea power upon the ruins of that of her rivals, friend and foe alike." That this should have been the case, as it incontestably was, will perhaps not surprise our readers. Mahan's judgment is all the more interesting, as its author is an enthusiastic admirer of Great Britain and all her deeds. In fact, according to him, an unassailable British world-empire is something so supremely magnificent, that all means are justified in order to create it.

It was in the first years of the War of the Spanish Succession that England stole Gibraltar—an event of far-reaching importance. This event did not mean a return to the Continental policy of the Plantagenets, but merely proved that England had risen to the rank of the first maritime Power—it embodied in a concrete manner England's claim to rule the seas. Henceforth her aim was to secure as many naval stations as possible; and this aim could not be realised otherwise than at the expense of the Continental nations. The latter, as far as they possessed coasts, were in future to be perpetually menaced by the guns of the English fleet. France had coveted Spain; but it was England who stole Gibraltar, which commands the entry into the

Mediterranean. This act of robbery was the second of the decisive steps taken with a view to ensuring England's supremacy in the last-named sea.

Another important event which took place during that period was a treaty of commerce, which England concluded with Portugal—the so-called Methuen Treaty. England had wisely allied herself with weak Portugal; for the latter was a large, albeit defenceless, colonial Power. The Methuen Treaty was characteristic of English methods: on the one hand England conceded to Portugal a reduction of the English duties on Portuguese wines, etc.; on the other hand, she obtained for English goods the right of free entry into Portugal. An English historian has remarked concerning this treaty: "Our alliance with Portugal and the Methuen Treaty between them gave England the monopoly of Portuguese trade." The final result was that Portugal's industry was annihilated by English competition; Portugal was compelled to purchase everything for itself and its colonies from English producers! The exported products were shipped on English vessels, and thus did it come about that the entire carrying trade to and from the Portuguese colonies fell into English hands. It is a historical fact that the Methuen Treaty completed the irreparable ruin of Portugal. Concluded in 1703, it has obliged Portugal to remain England's obedient vassal down to the present day.

England's statesmen have therefore every reason to speak in the most caressing and loving way of their dear friend and ally Portugal!

It is not less interesting to consider the Assiento Treaty between Spain and England which was incorporated in the Treaty of Utrecht. The Assiento Agreement enabled England to import every year a certain number of negroes into the Spanish colonies; it gave her the further right of sending every year a trading ship to Portobello. In this way did England open for herself a market in the Spanish possessions, thanks to which the products of English industry could be despatched thither in ever increasing quantities. The Assiento Treaty shattered the Spanish colonial trade monopoly as effectively as the Methuen Treaty shattered that of the Portuguese. The great plan of Louis XIV had been to unite France, Spain, and Portugal in one vast Continental and Colonial Empire. The two treaties above mentioned show us clearly how this plan had collapsed, and how immense was England's profit—especially by comparison with England's sacrifices. The English losses in the naval war had been very small, and those on land had been smaller still; for the so-called "English" armies on the Continent, commanded by Marlborough, were not English at all, but German. England had sacrificed nothing but money, just as every business firm must advance the costs of foundation of a new enterprise. But such a firm knows beforehand that it will recoup those costs; so did England. She recouped them along with colossal interest, although her risks had been insignificant, seeing that the enemy could not possibly do her any great harm. The belligerents on the Continent, however, fought so desperately and so long for England's business interests, that over and above the profits already indicated, England was able to evict France from her settlements in India, Canada, and the United States.

It was the same old story: the Continental nations obtained for England, at the cost of their own blood and riches, the control of the seas and the predominant position as colonial Power. The English statesmen understood this perfectly well. We are told that William Pitt the Elder once said that he would conquer America on the battlefields of Germany.

CHAPTER IV
"WE HAVE CONQUERED CANADA IN GERMANY"
FREDERIC THE GREAT AND ENGLAND

William Pitt was one of the greatest statesmen that England ever produced, he was a man whom people never tire of praising for his noble-heartedness. Around the middle of the eighteenth century he expressed himself as follows: "France is chiefly ... to be dreaded by us in the light of a maritime and commercial power.... All that we gain on this system is fourfold to us by the loss which ensues to France.... Surrender (of St. Pierre and Miquelon) would enable her to recover her marine." This was, therefore, the point of view of that noble-hearted statesman, in whose opinion not nearly enough loss and humiliation had been inflicted on France. What England considered to be most particularly advantageous was the loss suffered by her rival. This was after the war of the Austrian Succession, during which England had employed Austria against France, according to her usual methods. Whilst France was busy with the war on land, England captured enormous booty on sea. Mahan tells us that the commerce of all three nations—France, Holland, and England—had suffered enormously; "but," he continues, "the balance of prizes in favor of Great Britain was estimated at £2,000,000.... France was forced to give up her conquests for want of a navy, and England saved her position by her sea power, though she had failed to use it to the best advantage." Mahan's last statement is correct, but this was more than compensated for by the fact that England possessed obliging Continental Allies, who took upon themselves to weaken France. As usual it was England's chief partner, i. e., Austria, who did the worst business; she lost Silesia, and a large part of Northern Italy (which she surrendered to the King of Sardinia); and she was compelled, as the result of these losses, to enter into her alliance with France.

While these sudden and unforeseen changes were taking place in the political system of Europe, English ships were chasing the French ones, and finally forced, by their unceasing attacks and vexations, the King of France to declare war.

This brings us to the part played by England in the Seven Years' War. In the opinion of the English statesmen, the moment had come to complete the theft of the French Colonial Empire. Too much had also remained of the French trading fleet. Six months before the declaration of war an English fleet sailed into the Bay of Biscay, and did not leave it before capturing 300 French trading ships, worth $6,000,000. Subsequently England blockaded the French coasts, and captured all the ships—belligerent or neutral—bound for French ports. Not only did the English recognise that the time of the harvest had come, but, with the unerring instinct of the bandit, they determined to reap the maximum. Frederic the Great waged with true heroism a long and desperate war on the Continent, in which he earned for himself immortal fame; only with great difficulty did he manage to safeguard the frontiers of his country, whereas England filled, thanks to him, the pockets of her shopkeepers. "Without the victories of the Prussian grenadiers there would be to-day no English world-trade": such is the verdict of Schmoller.

Frederic the Great was obliged to ally himself with England, and to accept English subsidies. He was fighting for the existence of Prussia, England—as usual—for her own purse; she knew that the subsidies were in the nature of an investment yielding immense profits. The result of the war was that England received Canada and Florida, besides the whole of the United States east of the Mississippi. Spain received from France the territory west of that river. In India, France renounced the right of exerting political influence. England's aim had been realised. Her booty on sea and oversea was colossal; whereas the Continental nations were exhausted by the loss of blood and money, and the distribution of territory in Europe remained almost the same as it had been previously. It is interesting to notice what Frederic the Great thought about his ally, England, during the Seven Years' War. It was clear to him, from the beginning, that England, if she wanted to do so, could render him very efficacious assistance—all the more so as Frederic had recognised the great error committed by France in giving up the fundamental principle of the policy she had hitherto pursued: namely, the energetic carrying on of the maritime war with England. Under these circumstances it was much easier for the latter to come to Prussia's help. "Nothing," we read, "was of greater importance to the King of Prussia at this time, than the news of the English preparations for a Continental war." History tells us what became of all these preparations.

Frederic's verdict concerning the part played by England is well known, and he has himself put it on paper: "When she concluded peace with France, England sacrificed Prussia's interests in the most shameless manner. She then committed an even more disgraceful breach of faith. She offered Austria the re-conquest of Silesia, and in return for this humiliation inflicted on Prussia the Court of Vienna was to be allowed to resume its former friendly relations with England. As if all this treachery were not yet enough, English diplomacy was busy in St. Petersburg trying to stir up a feud between the King of Prussia and Czar Peter III. So much malignity and so much open hostility destroyed all the links once uniting Prussia and England. The alliance, which common interests had concluded, was replaced by bitter enmity and intense hatred." From the very beginning of the war Frederic had rightly desired that England should send a fleet into the Baltic and bombard the port of Cronstadt. He attached the greatest value to such a manœuvre. But "England ruled the ocean and all the other seas; she cared, consequently, nothing for the Baltic or the Sound. She attached little importance to the measures taken by the three Northern Powers, whose ships barred the entrance to the Baltic. The English Admirals had taken Cape Breton (at the entrance to the Gulf of St. Lawrence), and had occupied the island of Gorea (on the African coast). India offered them every opportunity for conquests; and they would have had none on the coasts of Denmark, Sweden, and Russia.

"The great successes of the English in no wise diminished the weight of the burden borne by the King of Prussia, any more than they safeguarded his throne. He asked them in vain for a fleet to protect his Baltic ports, which were menaced alike by Russia and Sweden. The overweeningly arrogant English nation, which has hitherto been uniformly favored by luck, and which considers exclusively its own business interests, despised its allies as if they were mercenaries. England was perfectly indifferent to everything outside trade. Neither Parliament nor people paid the smallest attention either to the war in Germany or to Prussian interests. Everything that was not English was looked down on. The English were, in fact, such unreliable allies that they even stood in the way of the King during the negotiations, when common decency would have required them to support him." Frederic was here referring to his efforts to conclude an alliance with the Sublime Porte, in view of inducing Turkey to march against Austria. England obstructed these negotiations by all the means at her disposal, because she feared that an increase of Prussian influence in the Near East would entail an increase of Prussian trade.

Such was Frederic's opinion of his English allies, whose help he had been forced to accept owing to the extremely unfavorable circumstances in which he was placed. We will ourselves complete the information imparted by the Prussian King: during the war, and especially towards its close, England endeavored to negotiate with all the enemies of Prussia—not only with Austria and Russia, but also with France. She informed the Czar of her readiness to obtain from Prussia any territorial concessions which the former might wish for, and exactly at the same time she offered Austria Silesia; she also proposed to the French Government that the latter should, after the conclusion of peace, enter into possession of Wesel, Geldern, and the surrounding districts. We unfortunately lack space to discuss in detail the perfidious game then played by English statesmen. But the spectacle teaches us once more the time-honored truth, which is still ignored by some to-day, and which Frederic expressed by saying that the English care for nothing outside their own trading interests, and that they despise their allies as mercenaries. One can go still further, and say that England never really espouses the cause of another country, even when she is allied with it; such a country merely appears to her as useful for the moment, in so far as it serves

England's mercantile interests. These interests are not always to be found on the surface; but they are always at the bottom of every political combination entered into by the politicians in London. As soon as England, during the Seven Years' War, had reaped her own abundant harvest and was certain that the conclusion of peace could not in any way diminish her profits, she at once sacrificed without hesitation the interests of Prussia, and broke the treaty she had signed with Frederic. And yet, without Prussia and Frederic, England would never have been able to drive France either from North America or India! Had France not been weakened by the war with Prussia, the former would have been able to play a very different part on the seas. But all that counted for nothing. Prussia was not to be permitted to extend her boundaries, nor to increase her strength; France had been sufficiently weakened; as for Austria and Russia, they could, by means of skilful wire-pulling, be made to serve Great Britain's interests usefully. Consequently did England desire the prompt conclusion of peace. No one was allowed to gain anything by such a peace, except England.

Pitt had spoken truly, when he said: "We have won Canada in Germany." Although the Seven Years' War, with its oversea expeditions and its subsidies, had cost England a good deal of money; it was very soon seen that one of its first results was to bring about an astonishing development of all the branches of England trade and industry. In other writings of his, Frederic the Great has noted down this rise of prosperity, not without surprise; he remarks that the national debt was enormous, but that, on the other hand, the general level of wealth was extraordinarily high. After the war it was all the easier to reduce progressively the national debt, as an ever-growing income of gigantic proportions was accruing, not only to individuals, but also to the state—especially from India. But treasures and products of all sorts arrived also from all the other colonies. The British trading fleet ruled the seas; for the Royal Navy had conscientiously done its duty, and thousands of foreign trading ships—the property of enemies, neutrals, friends, and allies alike (for England is always delightfully impartial in these matters)—had disappeared. As usual, after a Continental war, industry, commerce (with the exception of a little coasting trade), and the entire force of production, were ruined. Under the influence of peace, the wants of the population asserted themselves once more; but its strength did not allow it to satisfy those wants itself, to build up a new trading fleet, to develop a new industry. England's industry did the work. It must also be observed that the capital wealth of Great Britain had immeasurably increased, and had assumed ever more and more the aspect of an octopus sucking the life-blood of the other European nations. The more numerous the wars which those nations were compelled to wage for England, the more crushing did England's superiority in this respect become. Ever less and less grew the competition capable of exerting an influence either on the selling or on the purchasing prices of English industry. Gold and raw materials flowed free of cost, and in an uninterrupted stream, into England; they either came from England oversea possessions, or from Spanish and Portuguese colonies, the exploitation of which England had reserved by treaty to herself. Thus was business doubly profitable. We must also remember that the great majority of freights were shipped on board England vessels; and that in this way also money flowed into English purses.

During the Continental wars England acquired an immense colonial empire; that is to say, she robbed a quantity of territories belonging to other people, after having reduced the European nations to impotence on sea by stirring them up one against another. The same policy enabled England to acquire practically the whole of the shipping trade, and to establish herself as mistress of the seas.

France had lost many vitally important things, both in the shape of territory and in that of prestige. But the French only came to recognise the extent of their losses later on; and they soon forgot the lesson.

An interesting page in the history of the Seven Years' War is that which deals with the attitude of England towards Spain. France had signed a convention with Spain, with a view to obtaining Spanish assistance. This assistance was to be rendered a year after the signing of the agreement; it was thus in the nature of a long-term bill. England seized the opportunity to attack Spain, and to pounce with her usual vulture-like rapacity on the Spanish colonies and on Spanish vessels; she likewise continued her piratical forays against the French coasts. It was especially the silver cargoes which excited the greed of the pious English heroes of the sea. English historians still regret that Pitt's advice to attack Spain was not followed earlier. If it had been, many more "glorious" successes could have been obtained. Campbell wrote in his Lives of British Admirals the following exquisite passage: "Spain is just the country which England can always fight with the best chances of acquiring fame and success. Her immense empire is weak in its center-point; the sources from which help can be obtained are far away; and the Power which commands the sea will be able to obtain without difficulty the wealth and the commerce of Spain." We are here told candidly that an attack on the weak Spanish empire offered every prospect of success, and of the acquisition of fame (!). For this reason was Spain attacked at every possible opportunity, and her still wealthy and immense empire perpetually plundered. The center-point of that empire was weak. Spain's weakness resided in the fact that her sea power had been destroyed; she believed erroneously that local garrisons placed in the colonies would be able, by means of coast defences to maintain the cohesion of a great imperium. But between Spain and her colonies the British fleet had wedged itself in. In a similar manner was France separated from her oversea possessions. It was by means of robbery and piracy that England had developed into a world-Power at the expense of Europe.

CHAPTER V
THE PROTECTOR OF NEUTRAL COUNTRIES—THE LIBERATOR OF EUROPE
SECOND HALF OF THE EIGHTEENTH CENTURY

France set herself, with remarkable energy, to rebuild her fleet, which had been annihilated in 1759. But the decision came too late, and the errors of past years could not be repaired. Matters stood somewhat more favorably in the case of Spain; but England had long since forgotten to fear the Spaniards at sea, and rightly so, for the latter have never shown themselves equal to the English on the waters.

In the third quarter of the 18th century, began the American War of Independence; both in France and Spain the hope of crushing the pirate empire dawned again. This hope was destined to end in disappointment; once more was the Continent vanquished by the Island. True, England was often in difficulties, on account of the immense extension of the seat of war; but, as far as her struggle with France and Spain was concerned, it was in reality decided as soon as it began. A very important factor of English success and English strength in all these wars, was the skill with which England's statesmen and admirals invariably treated the Continent as a whole. We have more than once drawn attention to the fact that not only England's enemies, but also neutral countries, and even England's friends, had to suffer during a maritime war. Under the pretext of damaging the enemy, all trade was forbidden alike with hostile and with neutral ports; and the English captured impartially every ship that sailed the seas under foreign flag. This policy, consistently followed out, had the result of gradually eliminating the flags of all neutral and hostile countries, and of replacing them by the English flag. With special rigor had England maintained a claim first advanced by her during the Dutch wars: namely, that of seizing on neutral ships cargoes destined for the enemy. During the war between England, on the one hand, and France and Spain, on the other, neutral shipping in the North and the Baltic Seas had suffered greatly; for England did not wish France and Spain to obtain corn and wood from the countries bordering the Baltic. Thereupon France and Spain allied themselves with Russia, Sweden, and Denmark; and the "armed neutrality of the Baltic Powers" was proclaimed under Russia's leadership. Here at last we see an effort made by a part of the Continent to offer joint resistance to the monstrous claims and the insatiable greed of England, and to demand just and considerate treatment. The following concessions were required from Great Britain: immunity of the enemy's cargoes carried under neutral flag; arms and munitions alone to be contraband, and not foodstuffs nor wood for building purposes—provided they be not destined for the Government of a belligerent nation; neutral ships to have the right of going to the unblockaded ports of a belligerent country, and of carrying on trade along the latter's coasts; lastly, blockades to be only recognised when a sufficient naval force effectively bars the entrance to the blockaded port.

We need scarcely point out how closely the demands made by the neutral Powers in 1780 resemble those formulated in 1914–15. Not only does this hold good of the definition of the word "contraband"; but also of the demand that a harbor or a coast shall be considered as legally blockaded only when the blockade is effective, i. e. when a sufficient fleet is present to enforce it. This claim was raised, in 1780, against one of the worst of England's traditional methods of warfare. It had always been the custom of the English simply to declare a coast to be "blockaded"—even when no English ships were in the neighborhood. This was the so-called "paper-blockade," or, as the French called it, *le blocus anglais*: a most convenient invention! Such a method released the English fleet from all the duties incumbent on the blockading party; it permitted English trade to reap free of cost all the advantages of the blockade, e. g. the right of seizure of all vessels, neutral or hostile, etc.; it rendered the Continent wholly dependent on English ships for its sea communications. Concerning this question, and also concerning the other, to the effect that the neutral flag may cover cargo destined for the enemy or exported by the latter, England had been negotiating with the leading Continental Powers during more than a hundred years. England had often admitted the demands in question, but only in times of peace. When herself engaged in war, she despised such international agreements as much then as now.

One after another nearly all the Continental Powers, including Prussia, joined the Armed Neutrality League. When Holland decided to follow suit, England declared war on her, and the insatiable vulture flung itself on to the Dutch colonies. Mahan writes: "The principal effect ... of the armed neutrality upon the war was to add the colonies and commerce of Holland to the prey of English cruisers.... The possessions of Holland fell everywhere, except when saved by the French...."

At first, and as long as the American War of Independence lasted, England showed herself disposed to agree to the proposals of the League of Armed Neutrality. But she refused to allow the Baltic Powers to participate in the peace negotiations, and subsequently declared: the demands of the League, that is to say in substance the conditions of the Peace of Utrecht, hold good for the contracting parties exclusively! In this way were the very Powers excluded, who had been the first to protest against the unjust treatment of neutral nations. It was also proclaimed in the House of Commons that the doctrine concerning the "effective blockade" the limitation of the term "contraband" to war supplies, and the right of the enemy's cargoes to sail under neutral flag, were not considered by the British Government as in any way binding the latter for the future. Thus had the League of Armed Neutrality contributed to the development of a propaganda in favor of the recognition of certain principles of international maritime law; but it had achieved no practical result whatever. Ten years later the League itself was dissolved. England then succeeded in stirring up the Czaritza against revolutionary France. An agreement was drawn up, according to the terms of which a Russian fleet was assigned the task of preventing all communication between France and the neutral Scandinavian countries.

All these are events, the importance of which may appear to the reader, by comparison with the epoch-making occurrences of that period, to be insufficient to warrant their recounting in detail here. But none the less are they important. It was certainly of more than passing importance that the attempt made by all the neutral Continental Powers to ally themselves against the English pirate, and to obtain in this way recognition of the right of neutrals—that this attempt should have been vain. To-day the neutral countries are astonished and indignant at the matter-of-course manner in which Great Britain tramples all international law and custom under foot. They cannot understand that the only excuse alleged by her should be: it is unfortunately necessary that the neutrals be compelled to suffer, seeing that Germany, the chief enemy of Great Britain, must be crushed. About 130 years separate us from the period of the Armed Neutrality of 1780. Many international conferences have been held during these thirteen decades; many agreements have been made concerning the laws of maritime warfare, and especially concerning the right of neutral shipping in time of war. An immense quantity of books have been written on the subject; and in no other connection have we heard so much about the growing solidarity of civilised people being promoted by the increased means of communication. The nineteenth century, and the beginning of the twentieth, were periods in which international phrases were held in high honor. The European States—and not only the weaker ones—believed that a lot of printed paper was sufficient to suppress the Englishman's thieving instincts. They thought that it was enough to talk about rights, and duties, and solidarity; and that the civilised British nation had accepted the principle of the existence of a supreme international law, equally operative in times of peace and war. The disappointment was hence all the greater—but those who shared it got what they deserved. How could any reasonable person believe that methods systematically and successfully adopted during centuries—that the fundamental instincts of the English nation and the underlying principles of English policy: that all this would suddenly be abandoned, annihilated, simply because the Continental States hoped that it would be so, and talked about the possibility of it happening? In England people spoke a lot, and eloquently, about humanity and civilisation. But for every English statesman and admiral it was self-evident that, in war, everything would remain exactly as it always had been. It would be worth while to follow attentively the attitude adopted by England, throughout the centuries, not only towards the above-mentioned questions of maritime law, but towards a great many others, and to present the results of that inquiry to the astonished eyes of our readers. The latter would then perceive that, under altered forms, English aims and methods have remained invariably the same since the sixteenth century up till the present day. Maritime war is destined by Providence to serve the ends of the Chosen People; such wars are for them times of abundant harvest; and it is the duty of the English people, of its statesmen and admirals, to see that the Will of Providence is duly carried out.

The harvests reaped by England as a result of her pirate wars had always been substantial. But the greatest harvest of all, the reaping of which should be decisive in the influence—economic and political—exerted by it on Britain's future evolution, was still to come.

In 1789 the French Revolution broke violently out, on the occasion of the summoning of the States-General in Paris. Two years later, Louis XVI and his family were brought back to the capital as prisoners, their attempted flight having been intercepted. Hereupon the Continental Powers allied themselves against France with the avowed intention of "employing every means in view of enabling the King of France to consolidate freely, and without let or hindrance, the foundations of the monarchy." On behalf of Great Britain, William Pitt the Younger declared that he declined to intervene in any way in the internal affairs of another State.

The war against France commenced, and luck favored the French arms; after a short time the French troops entered the Austrian Netherlands, i. e. Belgium. At the same time the National Convention issued a decree, declaring the Scheldt to be henceforth open, in conformity with the law of nature. In order to enforce this decree without delay, and in such a manner as to remove all misunderstandings, a French fleet entered the Scheldt and blockaded Antwerp, already besieged by the army. This happened in November, 1792. Shortly afterwards the British Government declared that it would never see with indifference a French occupation of the Netherlands; and that it could not admit France's claim to act as general arbitress of the rights and liberties of Europe. On January 21st 1793 Louis XVI was guillotined; and a little later the French Ambassador in London received from the British Government a brief and very impolite notice, to the effect that he must leave London within a week. This was but the prelude to war between France and England.

From the outset it was perfectly evident that the British Government would seek to wage this war in the name of one of those high-sounding principles, by means of which England has invariably sought to cloak her real designs. Nothing could have been more welcome to English Ministers than the death of Louis XVI. Full of noble indignation, with heaving breast and flashing eyes, the old pirate of the seas rose to arms. France, it was said, must receive her punishment for the murder of the King and for the atrocities of the Revolution; in view of the terrible crimes committed it was wholly impossible for England to remain disinterested, as Pitt had promised. England sacrifices all egotistical considerations, and makes the cause of monarchical Europe her own. To-day we are better able to judge the utterances of English statesmen and of the English press; and we can imagine the superb virtuosity, the wonderful skill, with which the "interests of Europe" and the "atrocities of the Revolution" were exploited, in order to keep the Continental nations in the dark as to the real motives underlying England's intervention in the war. As a matter of fact, these motives were to be sought in the occupation of Belgium by French troops, and in the opening of the Scheldt. "It was not the execution of the King, but the conquest of Belgium, which drove England into war." The English historian Seeley goes still deeper into the question, when he says: "The fight for the acquisition of new markets for English goods at the expense of the growing French industry, was at once keener and more popular than the fight against the Revolution." Alexander von Peez and Paul Dehn, the authors of that excellent book *England's Vorherrschaft aus der Zeit der Continentalsperre*, comment as follows on Seeley's words: "Commercial jealousy was reinforced by political fear. France might be strengthened by the Revolution, even as England had been by her own revolutions in 1649 and 1689; and the former might, in consequence, become a very dangerous rival. The more prominent was the part played in the world by France, and the more did England consider herself injured and menaced. It was not the liberties of Europe that English statesmen regarded as threatened, but rather England's commercial and industrial monopoly." Every word of this statement is true.

England now proceeded to set all Europe in motion, in order to drive the French out of Belgium and to prevent the Belgian and Dutch sea-coast from falling into the hands of a rival naval Power. British gold flowed once more in an uninterrupted stream into Europe, as it always did whenever there was a probability of doing a really successful business "deal" on a large scale. Revolutionary France had indeed done everything that was necessary to provide England with the most admirable pretexts; for had it not abolished the Christian religion? Can we not imagine how the Englishman's pious heart must have swollen within him? For the sole purpose of protecting religion and morals England was only too happy to be able to give money! Nothing characterises better the great comedy—the background of which Europe would seem not even yet to have perceived—than the literature of the Revolutionary and Napoleonic Era. The noble-heartedness of the free and pious Englishman is sung to every tune; the *leitmotiv* is invariably furnished by the noble and generous nation which, albeit in safety on its island, endeavors with motherly solicitude to diminish the sufferings of the Continental peoples, and which, animated by the marvellous spirit of self-sacrifice, fights indefatigably the good fight for religion, freedom, and order.

It is necessary, now, to turn our attention for a short while to Belgium, and especially to the question of the Scheldt. The independence of the Northern Netherlands had been recognised by the Treaty of Westphalia (1648); the latter thus gave legal sanction to Holland's total separation from the powerless German Empire—a separation that had existed *de facto* for a very long time. The Southern Netherlands, i. e. Belgium, remained Spanish property until 1713, when they were handed over by the Treaty of Utrecht to Austria. This state of affairs continued to exist until the outbreak of the wars between France and the European Coalition.

The Treaty of Westphalia compelled Spain to give her consent to the closing of the Scheldt. The Dutch States-General had declared that, for Holland, this measure was one of vital importance; for if Antwerp were to become a great and prosperous port, Amsterdam and Rotterdam must necessarily suffer by it to a greater extent than Holland, with her small resources, could bear. Consequently was the Scheldt closed, Antwerp's trade was ruined, and a terrible blow was dealt at Belgium's prosperity. In reality, the closing of the Scheldt was due not so much to Dutch as to English influence. English statesmen had known for centuries what the result would be if Antwerp were to fall into the hands of a great Power; and that England's trade would certainly derive no advantage—to say the least—from the existence of a prosperous port at the other side of the Channel, at the mouth of the Scheldt, close to the Rhine, the Meuse, and the Thames. A more convenient maritime position, and better means of communication with an immense commercial hinterland, than those possessed by Antwerp, cannot be imagined; in those days, when railroads did not exist, the situation was even superior to what it is to-day. The closing of the Scheldt was equivalent, under these circumstances, to the drying-up of an unusually rich source of trade and wealth, and even sea power. The restless mind of the Emperor Joseph II understood this, and he decided to demand the re-opening of the river. Holland, backed up by England, resisted the demand; negotiations ensued, which lasted several years. Mahan remarks that "Again, in 1784, she (England) was forced to look with anxiety—less on account of Austria than of France—upon this raising of the question of the Scheldt. There was little cause to fear Austria becoming a great sea power now, when she had held the Netherlands three-fourths of a century without becoming such; but there was good reason to dread that the movements in progress might result in increasing her rival's sea power and influence—perhaps even her territory—

in the Low Countries." Mahan neglects to tell us how England's jealousy of Austria manifested itself at that time—just as it had done on previous occasions. At the beginning of the 18th century, Austria had founded an East Indian trading company in Ostend. As Alexander von Peez tells us, the enterprise flourished, and thereby excited naturally the envy and suspicion of the English. "England created difficulties for the Emperor on the Rhine, and at the same time despatched envoys to the Great Mogul in India, who represented the Emperor as the principal enemy of Mohammedanism. For this purpose, certain highly-colored descriptions of the battles of Peterwardein and Belgrade were given. Finally in 1727 the company was dissolved, as a consequence of English threats." We would remark that certainly no other European Power could have been maltreated and exploited by England, as Austria was; but then the German Empire of that time was not a Great Power!

Emperor Joseph II soon gave up insisting on the opening of the Scheldt, for other things occupied his restless mind. France paid him an indemnity; and her statesmen drew the conclusion that it was henceforth permissible for them to develop relations of intimacy with Belgium, and to sign a military and naval convention with the latter. This policy of France was directed against England; it showed that the French statesmen understood the real motives by which Great Britain was actuated. It is possible that they were also of the opinion that, in the event of the Belgian question becoming acute, it would be of the greatest importance for France if Belgium were not on England's side. This was in 1785; and during the following years English diplomacy did everything it could to win over Holland.

Such was, then, the position of matters when, in 1793, the attack of the European Powers on France resulted in the conquest of Belgium by French troops, and in the opening of the Scheldt.

At first sight it would seem as if there were a certain similarity between the attitude of England at that date, and her ultimatum to Germany in 1914. There is certainly some resemblance between the two attitudes, but there is also a fundamental difference—namely, that Belgium, in 1793, was Austrian territory; and Austria was at war with France. France sent her troops into Belgium in order to conquer the latter; and she sent her fleet to open up a port of incomparable commercial value. The French Government intended, from the beginning, to keep Belgium; in fact, the possession of the whole of the Netherlands had been for centuries one of the chief objects of the Kings of France—and such an object could not possibly be attained except by conquest. Austria had, in conjunction with the other Continental Powers, attacked France, and the latter was in her right in invading Austrian territory. The French Government subsequently declared that its troops would evacuate Belgium; but it is doubtful whether it would have permitted the

Scheldt to be closed again. The occupation of Belgium, however, together with the opening up of the river, afforded England a sufficient reason to declare war on France. Only a short time before this, the British Government had manifested the firm intention of not intervening in the Continental war; its desire had merely been to inflict, in accordance with its traditions, as much harm as possible on the shipping trade of belligerents and neutrals; and if the occasion had presented itself, it would have gladly seized a colony or a naval station belonging to one of the nations at war. English statesmen had judged a policy of "watchful waiting" to be the best—especially as the British fleet was at that time not quite equal to its task. But in those days of wooden ships, and in view of England's colossal resources, the defects of the navy could very soon be repaired.

In 1914 the German Empire was attacked by Russia and France. The German Government requested Belgium, an independent but neutralised country, to allow the German armies to march through Belgian territory; it gave, further, every necessary guarantee to the effect that no territorial acquisitions were intended; it pointed out that military necessities alone dictated its request, and it promised compensation for all damage done. It likewise undertook to pay cash for all the provisions needed by its troops. Great Britain at once agitated the spectre of Belgian neutrality, and declared that the entry of German troops into Belgium must entail a declaration of war by the London Cabinet. A short time afterwards documents were found in Brussels, which showed that England, France, and Belgium had entered into a military agreement in 1906 with a view to preparing a joint attack on Germany. Since that date, consequently, a neutral Belgium had *de facto* no longer existed. Belgium—and this is the chief thing to be noted—had become a British basis of operations in one of the strategically most important regions of Europe. The British Government had already in advance ascribed to Belgium, in the carefully planned-out future war against Germany, a part similar to that played by Portugal during the Napoleonic wars.

Some years ago Lord Curzon wrote that the necessities of Indian defence urgently demanded the occupation, by British troops, of all the countries bordering the Indian frontier, as well as the conquest of Arabia and the transformation of the Persian Gulf into an English lake; for all such countries, and also the Persian Gulf, were in reality nothing but the natural fortifications of India. In the same way does England, as a matter of principle, regard all those European countries whose coasts are washed by the North Sea, the Channel, and the Atlantic, as "fortifications" of the British Isles—and as forming also England's commercial hinterland.

In 1793, when the last great struggle between France and England began, Spain and the Netherlands were both considered, in London, to be British "fortifications"; Hanover being in British hands, it was also possible to consider Germany in the same light, whilst, in the North, Russia formed the background to the Scandinavian States. When we consider the various political and military combinations between 1793 and 1816 and when we abandon the historical legends invented concerning them, we shall see that France was the champion of the true interests of the Continent. England, and her following of European States, represented solely British insular interests, whereas Russia changed sides like a weathercock. This judgment in nowise diminishes the value of the German War of Liberation, but it certainly does call in question the traditional opinion to the effect that it was England who liberated Europe. The question as to whether England, as a matter of fact, contributed anything to that "liberation," remains an open one, even if it be admitted that she played an important part in causing the downfall of Napoleon.

With joyful and untiring energy did the English statesmen of that epoch labor to prevent the flames of war being extinguished on the continent. As far as England's interests were concerned, Europe could never be laid waste sufficiently. England's participation in the military operations was the traditional one. From the beginning, she considered the war as a maritime one (as far as she herself was concerned), poured oil on the flames in Europe, and paid subsidies—which were, indeed, more often promised than actually paid. Of course it is the Germans who have always spoken with the greatest admiration and gratitude of the "free nation's" superb struggle for the liberty of Europe against the Corsican oppressor!

Admiral Mahan, whom we have often quoted, who is a passionate admirer of Great Britain, and who only finds fault with his pets when they have not been unscrupulous enough to suit him—Admiral Mahan writes as follows about the part played by England in the Napoleonic wars: "For these reasons great operations on land, or a conspicuous share in the continental campaigns became, if not absolutely impossible to Great Britain, at least clearly unadvisable. It was economically wiser, for the purposes of the coalitions, that she should be controlling the sea, supporting the commerce of the world, making money and managing the finances, while other states, whose industries were exposed to the blast of war and who had not the same commercial aptitudes, did the fighting on land." The same author says in another place: "The thriving condition of the manufactures and commerce of England, protected from the storm of war ravaging the Continent and of such vital importance to the general welfare of Europe, made it inexpedient to withdraw her people from the ranks of labor, at a time when the working classes of other nations were being drained for the armies." Mahan, the admirer of England, has here unconsciously defined the part which British statesmen so artfully ascribed to the Continent: no English workman should be allowed to fight, for this would damage British industry. The Continental peoples were there to do the fighting! Mahan tells us that, on the Continent, industry had been rendered impossible by the war; and he forgets that the latter was systematically encouraged by England. From an economic point of view, an experience repeatedly made by England in former wars was confirmed: namely, that the money invested in the shape of subsidies was recouped with interest, and that the constantly increasing capital in the country paved the way for the flooding of the foreign markets with the cheap products of British industry. The last-mentioned phenomenon, again, permitted in later years of the humble attempts made elsewhere to develop a national industry being nipped in the bud. The Continent grew ever poorer, and England ever richer. With characteristic English hypocrisy could Pitt say, on the occasion of the reception of some expelled French priests: "The country that has welcomed those priests, is a country which Heaven has blessed. In the midst of the universal distress which has befallen other nations, Providence has permitted Great Britain to cover herself with glory and honor. Peace reigns in her palaces, her barns are full. All parts of the globe pay tribute to her industry, all the seas are marked with the sign of her victories." The same statesman said in 1801: "If we compare this year of war with former years of peace, we shall, in the produce of our revenue, and in the extent of our commerce, behold a spectacle at once paradoxical, inexplicable and astonishing; we shall see, that, in spite of the alarm and agitation which has often prevailed in the course of this arduous contest ... we have increased our external and internal commerce to a higher pitch than ever it was before; and we may look to the present as the proudest year that has ever yet occurred for this country."

Let us return to the year 1793. Trembling with indignation at the sight of the murder of the French sovereigns, and of the introduction of the religion of Reason; deeply incensed by the proclamation of the Republic, and fearing for the liberties of Europe, England flung herself—on the trade and industry of France. The latter was to be isolated from the rest of the world. The British Government declared that it was necessary to starve the French nation, by preventing the importation of corn. When we consider that France in those days had a much smaller population than she has to-day, whereas her soil was just as fruitful then as now, it is difficult to suppose that the starvation plan was a serious one. Some sagacious Germans recognised afterwards, when it was too late, the truth of the matter: the starvation of France was a pretext, the object of which was to hold up to England's continental allies a common aim to be realised, and to hide the real purpose of the English blockade from their view. The purpose in question was none other than the destruction of the entire industry of the Continent, for England succeeded in persuading the majority of European States to bind themselves over not to sell anything to France. In this way did they suppress their own export trade to that country; and the consequence was, that especially the German industry lost a valuable, nay indispensable, market. German industry was, in future, compelled to work at such a cost, that the cheaper English goods were able to flood the German market. We can observe here the time-honored English policy, which wages war only when large business profits are to be drawn from it. The more heterogeneous and complicated European political life grew, the more cunningly did England proceed. At the beginning of the last century she succeeded, by the simple means of a few high-sounding words, in inducing the whole of Europe to destroy the latter's own industry and the foundations of its own economic existence.

Thus began that colossal commercial war, which, for England, was the end-purpose of the military and naval operations. The French Republic replied to the English blockade by the exclusion of all English products, and by raising the French tariff. These protective measures proved very favorable to the industrial development of the country, and further efforts were made to stimulate such development by means of other economic reprisals. France applied to the neutral States for help in preventing the smuggling of English goods, all of which were confiscated. We need hardly say that the English did not remain inactive; and that they did not hesitate to denounce the absolutely justifiable retaliatory measures adopted by France, as an unheard-of crime against humanity. The English fleets exercised with greater rigor than ever their self-assumed duties as "policemen of the sea"; that is to say, they stole as many French and neutral ships as they could get hold of. They further compelled all ships coming from oversea countries to call first at an English port; this measure later on during the era of the Continental blockade was rendered worse by the imposition of heavy port duties on such vessels.

England's continental allies were chained hand and foot. On the one hand they had, as we already pointed out, bound themselves down at England's behest to destroy their own trade; on the other hand, she completed, in the most friendly manner, the ruin of their shipping. As far as they possessed any maritime trade, they likewise suffered from the French reprisals, directed against England. The neutral countries suffered scarcely less; they came at last, in 1800, to recognise that they had no possible interest in sacrificing their commerce and industry merely to please England. The Northern States concluded a new alliance on the ruins of the old Neutrality League of 1780. The question once more arose of the liberty of goods under neutral flag, and of the right of search claimed by England. The neutral countries were of opinion that the right of search, in the case of trading vessels accompanied by warships, should be negatived on principle. Several brutal attacks on Swedish and Prussian trading ships, and another on a Swedish warship, formed the last straw that broke the camel's back. Under Russia's leadership a new Armed Neutrality League was constituted in 1800. Its requests were both just and moderate: liberty of transport of all goods (outside contraband) under neutral flag; contraband to include henceforth munitions of war only; prohibition of the so-called "right of search" in the case of trading vessels accompanied by warships; liberty of travel for neutral ships, which are to be allowed to sail freely to the ports of belligerent nations provided no effective blockade exists.

These just claims roused the English to intense fury. The Government declared them to be not only hostile, but preposterous, disgraceful, insulting to English "supremacy." England would under no circumstances sacrifice her "rights" to the Jacobin principles now fashionable, and which had been derived from France.

The Neutrality League of 1800 insisted on its demands. Prussia, Denmark, and Sweden rallied around Russia, as leader of the neutral nations; energetic efforts were made to keep the Baltic and North Seas open for neutral shipping, and to close the Baltic to British shipping, as long as England should not agree to the just demands of the neutral Powers. We must bear in mind that the trade with Northern and Eastern Europe was of immense importance for England at that time; the countries bordering the Baltic constituted a rich market for British industrial products, and it was from them that England obtained very large quantities of corn and timber. Already at that time was Great Britain dependent to a large extent on the importation of foodstuffs for the feeding of her population.

The neutral Powers began their preparations for closing the entrance to the German rivers flowing into the North Sea and the Baltic. Hereupon England required Denmark to abandon the Neutrality League, and the claims put forward by the latter. Denmark was further required to open her ports without delay. The Danish Government refused to accept these demands; the result was the bombardment of Copenhagen by English warships, and an attack on the Danish fleet. Almost immediately before these events took place, the Emperor Paul, the leading spirit of the whole Neutrality movement, was assassinated in St. Petersburg. The history of this celebrated murder has admittedly never been cleared up; but when we consider it in the light of contemporary political happenings, we may take it for granted that the assassins of the Czar, and also the immediate instigators of the crime, were in the pay of the British Government. The crime in question must be laid to the charge of the pious and free English people—of the same nation which, in its virtuous indignation at the murder of Louis XVI, plunged Europe into a series of wars lasting 22 years. The assassination of the Czar and the bombardment of Copenhagen took place at such admirably calculated intervals, that the former could be made known in Copenhagen at the very moment when the British guns were opening their fire on the city. Denmark gave in, the Armed Neutrality of 1800 was at an end, and Russia concluded a separate agreement with Great Britain. The latter maintained all her claims with regard to neutral shipping intact.

Once more had the Continent been outwitted by England—and precisely that part of the Continent, which, had its various component elements kept together, would have constituted a by no means insignificant factor in politics. The League had come to grief owing to the double-faced attitude adopted by Russia—an attitude which the Empire of the Czars kept up during the whole of the Napoleonic wars. We cannot now discuss the numerous other aspects of the political situation at that time. But when we consider this situation impartially, we must come to the conclusion that an active co-operation of the nations forming the Armed Neutrality League with one another, together with a rapprochement between those nations and France, would have produced the happiest results for Europe. And not only that. The break-up of the Armed Neutrality League of 1800 marks another step in the development of England's sea power to the detriment of Europe. Once more the determination of the "mistress of the sea" to consider and to treat Europe exclusively as a land offering facilities for commercial enterprise, manifested itself. English statesmen spared neither trouble nor money in stirring up new wars on the Continent, and in endeavoring to induce the European nations to adopt such economic measures as might weaken them commercially and industrially. As a "reward" for their services, England coolly and unscrupulously destroyed the maritime trade of her friends—whether the latter were allies, or simply neutral.

England's struggle against the Armed Neutrality was in every way an offensive one. This is not only true of the bombardment of Copenhagen, or of the naval expedition to the Baltic Sea; but it holds good of the whole policy which led up to the acts in question. It is characteristic of the immense increase of England's strength, that she should have felt herself capable of pursuing such a policy. For it was one thing to send a fleet against Holland, or even against Spain; and quite another to despatch a fleet through the North Sea into the Baltic, which was closed in by mighty naval Powers. The energy of desperation with which England, by means of her fleets and the murderers suborned by her, fought the Northern Powers with beak and claw, proves how highly she rated the danger threatening her from that quarter.

CHAPTER VI
THE GREAT HARVEST
THE NAPOLEONIC WARS

German historians generally place the military aspects of the Napoleonic wars so prominently in the foreground, that the economic aspects of these wars are entirely overlooked. The Continental Blockade established by Napoleon is considered as the only event of economic importance. The truth is, however, that the military events were, to a much larger extent than is generally supposed, determined by economic causes. Peez and Dehn have reproduced an utterance of Lord Granville's, which the latter made in 1800 to the effect that Napoleon would derive from peace considerable advantages to the commerce, trade, and manufactures of the republic, whilst England would be left merely in its present situation. The noble Lord should have added that the future prospects for England's commerce and industry would have been considerably less rosy, had peace been maintained. Even Continental war—as we have seen again and again—filled English barns and purses alike. But as soon as peace returned, Europe recovered some of its strength, and endeavored to satisfy its own wants by means of its own efforts.

France was immoral and criminal enough to flourish thanks to the protection afforded by her tariff! Napoleon did not fulfil England's hope, that France would conclude with her neighbor at the other side of the Channel a treaty of commerce profitable solely to the latter. In general, Napoleon did not manifest the intention of placing his country in the service of Albion. The English waxed terribly indignant at such impertinence; and the entire nation was agreed that the power and wealth of the immoral French people must under all circumstances be broken. The most sacred rights of the Chosen People were menaced; and this implied, of course, that the liberties of Europe were jeopardised. Noble England wished to "save Europe from Napoleon." Needless to say she wanted no recompense—nay, she would even give of her own money for the purpose, in order to induce as many European nations as possible to participate in her glorious fight for liberty. The states which remained neutral sinned against Europe; and England was obviously fulfilling the behests of Providence in destroying their shipping and their industry. The time was past, when there was any reason to fear "armed neutrality." The English fleets ruled the seas, and blockaded the French and Spanish coasts—in fact, they blockaded, directly or indirectly, the entire Western coast of Europe. In the Mediterranean, Malta had fallen into English hands. Some years previously, Bonaparte's Egyptian campaign had failed. Its failure was inevitable, because the French fleet was insufficient; consequently the Egyptian Army was isolated, after Nelson had destroyed the French squadron at Aboukir. The lack of success of the expedition to Egypt signified a defeat of Europe at the hands of England. By way of the Pyramids, and with India as his goal, Bonaparte had intended dealing a heavy blow at Albion's power. He would have succeeded, if it had not been necessary for him to cross the Mediterranean. The matter would to-day be much easier for a Power placed directly or indirectly in a position to march from Turkish territory into Egypt. The analogy is a remarkable and a timely one! In order to realise the plan, it would only be necessary for the Turks to march against Egypt through the desert; or else an European Power, finding the road through the Balkan Peninsula open, would itself send troops to the Egyptian frontier via Turkey. If these conditions should one day be realised, England would have no arms wherewith to defend herself against the Continent; she would have no means wherewith to defend Egypt and India, or her world-power in general. She could fill the seas with her ships, she could bombard coasting towns and sink the enemy's vessels—but it would be of no avail. Sea power is in the long run impotent, when it is limited to the surface of the waters.

Napoleon's unsuccessful Egyptian undertaking was not, at bottom, an attack on England, but a measure destined to safeguard France's position in the Mediterranean. Nature has given France far more rights in those waters than England. We must also remember that Great Britain, by a series of wars of aggression, during which the European nations had been forced to do her business for her, had driven France and French trade from India.

Napoleon had failed in Egypt, but his determination to protect the position and interests of France, at home and abroad, by all the means in his power, against Great Britain—this determination was stronger than ever. Never has a Continental monarch or statesman recognised so clearly and completely the essence and the methods of English policy, as Napoleon. He knew that, for England, trade is the beginning and end of everything. He saw through all the masks and disguises which she had always put on, from the very first day when she had begun to consider Europe exclusively as a territory to be exploited in England's interests. He knew well the strength of his mortal enemy, and he knew also that the French fleet could not, either as regards quantity or quality, compare with the British. England, on the other hand, was aware that Napoleon was capable of becoming a terribly dangerous foe on the seas, if only she were to give him time. This is one of the chief reasons why she left him no leisure, why she stirred up one war after another against him, why she looked upon every day of peace as constituting an increased danger for herself. Napoleon was likewise acquainted with this fact; hence his efforts to establish peace in Europe. He had recognised in England the firebrand of the Western world; and he knew that she had systematically carried on arson as a trade for the last 200 years. Unlike the statesmen of other European Powers, and unlike a large number of Germans who, a hundred years later, fell from the clouds of dreamland when England declared war on us in 1914—Napoleon was to be deceived by no phrases or attitudes.

When England recommenced war in 1803, Napoleon resolved to attack the hereditary enemy on his own soil—in other words, to cross the Channel with an army of invasion. The plan, as is well known, was frustrated by the battle of Trafalgar, when Nelson destroyed the allied fleets of France and Spain. Henceforth was France's chance of obtaining even a temporary command of the Channel gone. What remained of the French navy lay bottled up in the harbors of the Atlantic coast. We must not take Napoleon's boast, to the effect that "six hours' command of the sea would have made him master of the world," too seriously. But on the other hand, the possibility is not to be denied, that a landing might none the less have been rendered feasible by a happy combination of circumstances. The problem of landing troops in large numbers on English soil was at that time much less complicated than it is to-day. The sailing ships which formed the navy of friend and foe alike, were at the mercy of wind and weather. Twenty-four hours without any wind might possess decisive importance for the success of a landing expedition. The speed of ships in those days was very small, and the range of their guns was insignificant by comparison with that of modern artillery. Frigate could only fight against frigate at a very short distance, whereas a naval battle can to-day be fought while the vessels are a long way from each other. Mines and torpedoes, submarines and airships, were then unknown. When we take all the new methods of warfare into consideration, it is evident that the transporting of troops over the Channel is to-day infinitely more dangerous; and, on the other hand, it is far more difficult to protect the transports. In addition to this, we must recollect that large masses of troops would be required, in order to permit a successful landing developing into a fruitful military operation. The invading army must be sure of receiving reinforcements without interruption; otherwise it would be infallibly doomed to early perdition in the hostile country. An uninterrupted supply of reinforcements presupposes lasting command of the Channel. Another factor has also to be borne in mind: the population of Great Britain has enormously increased during the last 110 years. The island is filled with munitions of all descriptions. A large number of men capable of bearing arms is available; and even if the overwhelming majority of them have no military training, yet they are capable of shouldering a rifle, and they know every corner of their country. Movements of troops in England are easy to effect in this age of railroads, cables, and telephones; and they can take place with a rapidity which would render the ulterior development even of a successful landing operation a far more difficult affair than it was in Napoleon's time. As matters stand to-day, there is no doubt that the population of England would form a single vast body of franc-tireurs, who would carry on the war against the invading army by all the means available, and to the bitter end. These necessarily brief reflections show us that a landing of troops in Great Britain is possible only if the invading Power possess, in one way or another, effective command of the sea. If this be not the case, then all plans of invasion are illusions—and illusions that are liable to become a source of danger.

As to whether Napoleon really believed it possible to realise his plan of invading England, after the French fleet had been destroyed at Trafalgar is an open question. Did he think it possible to rebuild the navy, and to train the necessary crews? We may consider it probable or improbable, as we like. But at all events the feasibility of the plan, from the military point of view, is incontestable.

The battle of Trafalgar made England the uncontested mistress of the seas, and ensured for her that supremacy which she maintained up till 1914. When the epoch-making battle in Spanish waters, amidst the scenes of former British piratical activity, was decided, Great Britain had attained her object. She could now take everywhere what she wanted. No one was in a position to oppose her, with the single exception of the United States of America, her former colony. The importance of Trafalgar was first properly appreciated at the end of the nineteenth century, and it was then exaggerated by some writers. All historians are in agreement upon one point: namely, that Napoleon's chances of success were not destroyed in Russia or at Waterloo, but at Trafalgar. This is none the less doubtful; for Trafalgar did but give England the supremacy over the seas, and frustrate for the time being Napoleon's plan of invasion. If, during the German War of Liberation in 1813, there had been no Blücher nor Gneisenau, no Bülow, nor Yorck, but only generals such as Schwarzenberg and Bernadotte, Napoleon would never have been defeated. If the winter of 1812 had not been so abnormally cold, it is possible that the Russian campaign might have ended differently. It is, consequently, not exact to regard the battle of Trafalgar as alone decisive in sealing the fate of Napoleon. Of course, England has never ceased to represent Nelson and Wellington as the saviors of Europe, which, it is said, they liberated from the "tyranny of the Corsican." The Continent was saved once more by England, who had spent "blood and money" for the ideal of liberty, for the expulsion of the tyrant, and for the maintenance of the principles of Legitimacy. Even to-day there is no Englishman who does not consider it to be the sacred duty of every European to accept this view of the matter.

Gourgaud and others tell us that Napoleon, at St. Helena, said that his greatest mistake had been to believe it possible to unite permanently all the nations of the Continent within a single empire. And here we have certainly the nucleus of the whole question. It was this mistake which caused

Napoleon's downfall. The forces inherent in every nation would certainly have asserted themselves, at one time or another, with elementary and irresistible violence, even without Trafalgar or the Peninsular War. It was the consequences of the same mistake which gave England her lasting victory. She would not have gained it, if Napoleon had not endeavored to permanently crush and join together all the peoples of Europe. Let us try and represent to ourselves France within the boundaries traced for her by the Congress of Vienna, and governed by Napoleon; after ten years of peace and systematic preparation, she would have been in a position to fight England on the seas with every prospect of success. A country possessing the coast and the natural wealth of France would undoubtedly, if left in peace, have developed strength enough to make her equal, if not superior, to Great Britain. This truth is not often grasped at the present day; but Frederic the Great had recognised it when he said how foolish it was of Louis XIV to make of the Continent the center-point of his wars, instead of devoting all his resources to fighting England. The great Prussian King admitted that the methods of warfare adopted by the English were, from the standpoint of the latter justifiable; the English concentrated their entire force on the sea, and entrusted the European nations with the task of weakening France on land. Napoleon would not have committed this error of Louis XIV, for he knew England too well. His own mistake was that of believing in the permanence of his conquests. Thanks to these conquests was England able to find States ever ready to fight for English trading interests.—What we have just said represents, of course, only the point of view of France a century ago.

According to English writers and orators, Trafalgar is supposed to have "saved Europe"! To-day, after more than a hundred years have passed, it is possible to ask the question as to whether the consequences of Trafalgar for Europe have in reality been so salutary. If we take the view that Napoleon's World-Empire would, for the reasons indicated by Napoleon himself, have collapsed in any case one day or another; we can, in truth, not discover a single consequence of Trafalgar which has been favorable for the Continent. Trafalgar it was which ensured for England the absolute supremacy on the seas.

When Napoleon had been compelled to give up his plan of invading England, and to turn his attention to Austria, he knew that for the immediate future he had no means wherewith to fight the Islanders directly. English historians, and also Mahan, have rightly recognised that everything henceforth undertaken by the Emperor against his chief enemy was in the nature of enterprises embarked on *faute de mieux*. This remark holds good of the Continental Blockade instituted by the Berlin Decrees. The famous blockade is extremely interesting to consider, for it shows us clearly the war between Napoleon and England in its true light—namely, as a war between

England and the Continent. The fundamental idea on which the blockade was based, was derived from the measures taken by the French Republic at the end of the preceding century—measures, the object of which was to prevent the French market from being overflooded by English goods. These measures were destined as a counterblast to those taken (long before the French Revolution) by England against enemies and neutrals alike. Such English blockades had been organised in every single maritime war waged by England; their object was, in part, to damage the trade of the adversary, but chiefly to benefit her own trade and shipping. The weapon had been found so useful, that the leaders of the Chosen People decided that they could not apply it often enough. With a view to extending its application still further, recourse was had to the "paper" blockades, wherever an effective blockade could not be maintained.

The measures taken by the French Republic towards the close of the eighteenth century, and which had been confined to France alone, furnished Napoleon with the idea of the colossal European blockade against English goods. A *conditio sine qua non* of the success of that blockade was that it should be applied *quod ubique et quod omnibus*—that not a link should be missing in the vast chain of prohibition. The English were cunning enough to understand this at once; and they therefore directed all their efforts towards breaking as many links as possible. The whole of the European coasts, from the Baltic to Gibraltar and the Eastern Mediterranean, were declared to be closed; they were to form a single impenetrable wall against all English products. Napoleon employed also the Northern States for this purpose—especially Denmark, who possessed the key to the Belt and the Sound. Thereupon an English squadron suddenly appeared before Copenhagen in 1807, and demanded of the absolutely neutral Danish State that it should surrender its fleet! England pretended that she wished to take the latter under her protection, and that she would give it back again later on. Denmark refused; the English promptly bombarded Copenhagen from the sea, and despatched also an army against the city. Denmark was forced to capitulate; and the whole of her fleet, consisting of 33 ships, was taken over by the English Admiral, and brought to England. The ships were all of them without crews; this proves beyond a doubt that Denmark was attacked in the midst of peace, and had no intention of abandoning her neutrality. As to whether Napoleon would have induced Denmark to abandon her neutrality later on, is another question. He had just come to an agreement with Czar Alexander I at Tilsit, and had drawn up with him the outlines of a sort of general partition of Europe. According to this scheme, Denmark was to be granted a considerable increase of territory at the expense of Northern Germany, in the event of her allying herself with France. Thus it was intended to make an offer to Denmark; but there was not the slightest evidence of any intention on the part of the latter to give up her neutrality, much less of any hostile preparations. Denmark was wholly defenceless when attacked by England, and this attack was nothing but a vile and dastardly act of brigandage. England, at the same time, stole Heligoland from the Danes, and the island became a basis of operations for the English smugglers on the North Sea-coast.

The crime of Copenhagen was in so far profitable to Napoleon, that it obliged Russia to declare war on England. After the seizure of the Danish fleet, the Baltic was at the mercy of the English; whereas up till now Russia and Denmark had been united by the bonds of a natural solidarity, resulting from their respective geographical positions. But Russia's efforts to repair the breach made in the wall erected against English importations, were vain. A second breach was made in the wall in the South. Napoleon's unskilful and psychologically false treatment of the Spanish nation caused a guerilla war to break out in the Peninsula. This war has become celebrated; but what is less well known, is that Spanish blood was shed in order to further English interests. Spain was ruined, her soil devastated; and when Napoleon's power in the country was definitely broken, the latter found itself tied hand and foot to England, dependent on English industry and English financial assistance. At the very moment when England hypocritically pretended to be fighting in Spain "for Spain and Europe"—at that very moment she achieved the last, decisive victory over the land of Cervantes, and trampled the erstwhile greatest nation of the West under foot. The same fate had previously overtaken England's vassal Portugal.

Napoleon's intentions were evident: Spain was for him but a means wherewith to fight England on the Continent. The Spanish and Portuguese coasts were to be closed to English products, as much as the Northern ones were. Napoleon likewise intended taking Gibraltar by means of a land attack. Viewed as a whole, the plan was at once a bold and a simple one: England was to be completely ostracised, and all possibility of selling anything to the Continent was to be withdrawn from her. Napoleon thought that the English would not be able to hold out for long under such circumstances—riots would break out, money would be scarce, etc. The immediate "preventive" measures taken by England against Denmark, Spain, and Portugal, showed that the British Government by no means underestimated the possible consequences of the European blockade. The Continental nations, for Napoleon, were so many instruments to be used in fighting England; the latter, on the other hand, used them as weapons against the French Emperor. But amidst all political changes, the Continent remained, for England, the territory to be exploited in the interests of her trade. The more the Continent was devastated and impoverished, the better it was for Albion; for thereby was the market assured for British producers. And when British warships captured or sunk the vessels of those States which were compelled reluctantly to obey Napoleon's orders—this was, of course, done in the interests of "European freedom."

The Franco-Russian friendship did not last long, after having reached its culminating point at the Congress of Erfurt in 1807. The two Emperors had progressed further with their scheme for the partition of Europe; but they had not, apparently, come to an agreement regarding Constantinople. Then came Talleyrand's betrayal of both Russia and England. When the separation of Russia and France finally took place, the Continental Blockade was at an end. None the less did England continue her old system; and, in 1809, she managed to drive Austria-Hungary into a war which ended disastrously, seeing that Austria was not ready, and had to stand up alone against France and Russia. It is possible that England may have feared a rapprochement between Austria and the two last-mentioned Powers; but it was in any case not creditable for the Austrian diplomatists, that they should have allowed themselves, after so many experiences, to be once more made the puppets of England. However, with the exception of Russia, no Continental Power had reason to be proud of its diplomatists!

In view of the war raging at the present day, it is not without interest to examine briefly the organisation of the struggle between Napoleon and England, from the technical and military standpoint.

Napoleon thought it possible to bring about the economic downfall of Great Britain; he therefore forbade all the countries under his sway or influence to do any trade with the latter. An army of French officials was placed all along the coasts—in fact, a main characteristic of the Continental Blockade was, that it existed solely on land, and not on the seas, which would have been the normal way of doing things. But England ruled the seas in the fullest sense of the word, and herein lay *ab initio* an important source of weakness for the whole undertaking; for it was impossible to close up effectively so long and irregular a coast. Napoleon himself admitted that not the smallest fishing-boat could go out to sea, without the English capturing it. The British Government, by way of reprisals, blockaded every port in which the Berlin Decrees were enforced. It further prohibited all neutral ships from trading with such ports; at least neutral ships could only obtain permission to do so, if they had beforehand visited a British port, where they had to pay a heavy duty and to take a cargo of English goods on board. Consequently did every neutral ship which entered a Continental harbor "break" the French blockade. Napoleon replied by ordering the confiscation of all neutral vessels which thus complied with the English regulations. Later on another step in the same direction was taken, and all English goods found on the continent were seized. We need not dwell upon the consequences of all these measures for the sea trade. The French shipping trade, which had re-flourished in spite of all wars, disappeared completely with the exception of an insignificant coasting trade. France was cut off from her colonies, and the latter were compelled to purchase all the goods and foodstuffs they needed from the United States. Owing to the interruption of all communications with her colonies, France lost the lucrative colonial produce trade, which had been hers down to the time of the English blockade.

The Continental blockade was not without creating difficulties for England; in the first place, enormous quantities of unsaleable goods were accumulated in the country; on the other hand, the raw material, which Great Britain imported from Europe, arrived only in extremely small quantities. Trade and industry suffered naturally, but the groans that could be heard were much louder than the sufferings in question were great. The English seized every opportunity to let themselves appear as the martyrs to the cause of Europe; whereas, in reality, the Continent was enduring martyrdom for the sake of England's greed. England was in the position of a rich and dishonest partner, who willingly risks a large sum in an enterprise, because his experience tells him that the business to be done, and which will ruin his associates, will bring him in colossal profits. The harvest is some little time in coming, and in the meantime matters do not always go smoothly; so he groans and whines, in order to make believe that he is undergoing agony, and that he is honest.

The English smuggling system was carried on on the very largest scale; in addition to this, there came the port duties on neutral ships, of which we have already spoken. In passing, we may observe that these port duties imposed on neutral vessels show with particular clearness the measurelessly arbitrary methods of dealing with foreign trade, adopted by Great Britain. She even went farther still: the same ships, on returning to their home across the seas, were obliged to call at an English port and to submit to being searched. As a matter of fact, the poor neutral countries have not been treated any better during the present war. But this is by the way. The main consideration for England was, not to impede neutral shipping, but to destroy it. The effect of the English blockade on the German States, can best be understood if we give a few examples. Owing to the blockade of the Hanoverian coast and of the mouth of the Elbe, the Silesian linen industry was almost entirely destroyed. The linen could no longer be exported by way of Hamburg; and the exporting of it through other ports proved so expensive, that foreign countries—especially England, America, and Spain—were obliged to seek a cheaper source of production. Prussia, who was entirely impotent, and whose statesmen were simple enough to suppose that the destruction of one of the leading industries of the country was not desired by England—Prussia protested in London against the closing of the Elbe. The same fate overtook Prussia's woollen export trade. Later on, after the fall of Napoleon, when the blockades disappeared and shipping became free again, Prussian industry found all its markets absorbed by English industry.

In addition to all this, England was at that time the only Power possessing a trading fleet; with the result that the European States had to pay her a further tribute in the shape of freight. The through transit from South to North Germany ceased altogether. In the whole of Germany the standard of living diminished, the State revenues sank in a truly disquieting manner, and everything was at a low level. The genius of Napoleon discovered, for France and the conquered countries, means whereby industry and commerce attained a surprising development in a short time. He also lessened, for these regions, the inevitable hardships inflicted by the blockade, by awarding so-called licences; he subventioned, in the most difficult days, industrial undertakings with cash, and in this way succeeded in creating a prosperity which exerted its salutary influence on various branches of industry and trade in Germany. But precisely these branches were subsequently ruined after the break-up of the Continental system and the fall of Napoleon; for then the vast quantities of goods accumulated in England overflooded the European, and especially the German, markets, and effectively crushed all competition.

English politicians of those days, and also later on, often raised their eyes piously to Heaven, and declared sanctimoniously that God had been exceedingly good to England; for He had permitted her to become ever richer and richer, and had saved her from the fury of war which had devastated the unfortunate continental countries. There was, certainly, a certain depression among English business-men at times, during the Continental Blockade. This is comprehensible; for all business-men are not equally far-sighted, neither are they always strong-minded. The tests to which they were put, were often hard; and if Napoleon had been in a position permanently and absolutely to close all the coasts of Europe, it may well be doubted whether England could have survived. The Continent, on the other hand, would have been able to do so, had Napoleon not abandoned his principle of ruining the States subjugated by him—and notably Prussia—for the benefit of France.

The War of Liberation resulted in the yoke, which Napoleon had imposed on Europe, being thrown off. The European nations were once more free. In those days, when the national spirit, long held in check, rose again unfettered, they knew not that another yoke had been laid upon them, the weight of which they were soon destined to feel—and to feel more and more with each advancing year: namely, the yoke formed by Great Britain's industry, and by her uncontested command of the seas. The position of England, alike as an European and as a World-Power, was indeed, at the time of the War of Liberation, an unique one. The Continent, to a large extent a mere series of battlefields, had been completely ruined by loss of life, by economic impoverishment, by political anarchy. An extraordinary wave of idealism had permitted the poorest of all continental countries, Prussia, to accomplish the most difficult of all tasks. Prussia fought for liberty, and sacrificed everything for it. The land of the Chosen People had not been profaned by the presence of the enemy. England had suffered scarcely any loss of life during the Napoleonic wars, outside that of some hundreds of men in the naval battles. Very few English had fought on the Continent—but all the more Germans! In Spain, England had made the Spaniards fight, besides the Germans. From a military point of view, in fact, England had done nothing at all. An expedition which she had despatched to Antwerp, failed miserably in its attempt to take the city. But even in this case, the British Government could truly say that everything necessary had been done to save the precious blood of Englishmen.

Napoleon had not, from the outset, menaced the existence of England as an independent Power and as a seafaring nation. His attempts to effect a landing in the island, and subsequently to exhaust the resources of the English by means of the Continental Blockade, were purely defensive measures. England it was who began the attack on France, for reasons which—as is always the case with such English attacks—were based on trading interests. It was in order to consolidate and develop her empire of the seas that England continually fanned the flames of war in Europe during twenty years—and at the end of that time she came proudly forward as the "liberator of Europe"! The simple-minded Germans believed it; and there are some who still believe it to-day. Innumerable historical works prove this, and endeavor to make out that we owe an incalculable debt of thanks to England for having safeguarded the liberty of the nations. There is, in fact, a legend circulated in Germany, to the effect that the English of those days were entirely different to their descendants to-day. Other people, again, are of opinion that the "golden age" of liberty-loving Britain came to an end with the wars of the Revolution; but they are firmly convinced that such an age existed prior to that date. The one view is as erroneous as the other. The methods and aims of the English nation have remained exactly the same, from the day when England, as an "island," was definitely differentiated from the "Continent"—when, in consequence, the egotistical interests of the former entered into conflict with the interests of Europe.

CHAPTER VII
ENGLAND DIGESTS HER BOOTY—THE CONTINENT GRADUALLY BECOMES UNRULY
1815–1890

England did not wish to leave the Continent any time to organise resistance to her commercial policy. Once Napoleon had been rendered harmless—in fact from the very moment when the battle of Waterloo developed into a great Prussian victory—we find her alongside of France. England restored to France the latter's King, who had resided on English soil; she concluded the long-foreseen agreement with Talleyrand; and thus, in conjunction with Russia, did she re-arrange the map of Europe. It was customary in Prussia in those days, and it is still customary to-day, to criticise the incapacity of the Prussian representatives at the Congress of Vienna, and to repeat the words of Blücher: "the pen has gone and lost everything which the sword had won." In itself, the criticism is perfectly justified; but the responsibility for what took place at the Congress of Vienna cannot be ascribed solely to the Prussian diplomatists. The fact of the matter was that the Great Powers wished neither a strong Prussia nor a strong Germany to arise. The letter written, before the War of Liberation, by Baron Stein to the Earl of Munster (the British statesman), appears to us to-day almost touching in its simplicity: "My desire is to see Germany great and strong, so that she may regain her nationality and her independence, and maintain them in her position between France and Russia." But that was just what no single European Power desired, least of all England. For the latter knew that a strong, united Germany would constitute an important factor in the world's industry, and would no longer be at the mercy of English manufacturers and merchants. It must be noted, further, that the spectacle of another nation growing in strength and prosperity has always been extremely distasteful to the Englishman. At first the English diplomatists let the Sovereigns of Europe amuse themselves with discussions concerning Legitimacy; for in this way could the nations be deceived as to their real interests. "Legitimacy" proved itself to be something excellently adapted to the interests of France—and of France only; thanks to the wonderfully skilful use made of this new rallying-cry by Talleyrand, the land of Napoleon was able, despite its defeat, to take up a relatively strong position. England, whilst pretending to be wholly disinterested, kept Malta and Gibraltar; but she gave back a few colonies to France. All the more energetically did England insist upon the territories which border the North Sea and the Channel being distributed in the manner most agreeable to her. Prussia was compelled to hand over her ancient province East Frisia to Hanover, the latter being, we must remember, a sort of English fief on the Continent. Prussia was thus without a single port on the North Sea. England further succeeded in persuading the Congress of

Vienna, through the agency of the Duke of Wellington, to unite Holland and Belgium—under the pretext that Belgium, left to herself, would be crushed by France. The British Prince Regent hoped in this way to bring both countries entirely under England's influence. The fact that the Belgian provinces had formerly belonged to the German Empire was, of course, wholly ignored; and much less still did it occur to anyone to revise the Treaty of Westphalia. Under England's influence—which remained, however, as unobtrusive as possible—the Congress succeeded in shutting Prussia off completely from the North Sea, albeit without Prussia Napoleon would never have been crushed. Prussia was placed, as a result of the decisions of the Congress, in so unfavorable a geographical position, that she was nearly rent asunder into two separate parts; the task of defending her frontiers in West and East was thus rendered as difficult as could be. Denmark kept Schleswig-Holstein, and basked once more in the sun of England's favor; for she henceforth held Prussia in check, seeing that she commanded the entry to the straits. Each of the States forming the German *Staatenbund* was granted the widest possible autonomy, in the well-founded belief that this was the most efficacious way of preventing the formation of a United Germany.

For all these misfortunes, the Prussian diplomatists were less responsible than the European Powers under England's leadership, all of which were interested in preventing the development of a strong Prussia and of a united Germany. The shutting off of Prussia from the North Sea was a far-sighted and highly important manœuvre on the part of England. The unification of Holland and Belgium under England's "guardianship" held out the prospect of still more important consequences. We have followed up the development of England's policy towards both those countries ever since the Dutch war of independence against Spain; and we have noted England's uninterrupted efforts to prevent them from getting on intimate terms with any of the seafaring Continental Powers, the reason being that the Dutch and Belgian coasts are washed by the North Sea and the Channel. In the Treaty of Vienna England tried to go another big step forward, and to convert the Independent United Netherlands into an outer fortification of the British Isles. It would be more correct to say that Belgium, and especially Antwerp, was to become a basis of operations on the Continental side of the Channel for a British invading force. Had this plan proved itself, in the course of time, susceptible of realisation, Great Britain would have had, not only as an insular but also as a continental Power, an incomparably strong position. Guardian of the United Netherlands, she would have been far less vulnerable than she was in the days of yore, when she conquered Northern France. For in the case of the Netherlands there would have been no question of conquest; the Netherlands would have become England's vassal, whilst retaining their independence.

However friendly she might be with France, England took her precautions in the South of Europe. The Sardinian question was settled in accordance with English wishes, and the Republic of Genoa was united with the Kingdom. In this way did England succeed in erecting a barrier against France on the one hand, and against Austria on the other; a barrier was likewise erected at the same time between France and Austria. Sardinia was obliged to rely always on British help, and the port of Genoa constituted the link between the Kingdom and Great Britain. In addition to all this, England's power in the Mediterranean was well assured by the possession of Malta.

Great Britain's world-position was greater, stronger, and more influential, than ever, after the Napoleonic wars. Her warships ruled the seas, and no other nation could even think of challenging British maritime supremacy. The British fleet was regarded as not only invincible, but as irresistible. Europe had been persuaded that her "liberation" was due to that fleet. For the first time for many centuries, England had no "enemy" on the Continent, for the simple reason that she needed none. The weakened and exhausted Continent lay at the mercy of John Bull, and the latter did not hesitate to exploit it. Especially was this the case with the German States, which were separated from each other by a wall of prohibitive tariffs, but whose markets were unreservedly open to foreign countries. France was clever and experienced enough to continue protecting her industry even after the fall of Napoleon. In this way did the break-up of the Continental Blockade have a destructive effect on the industry of several German States, during many years; all the more so as the English Government and English merchants alike had recourse, with their usual absence of scruples, to corruption and other dishonorable means for crushing German industrial competition *ab ovo*. The superstitious veneration which was entertained in Germany up till a comparatively recent date for all "genuinely English" products, dates back, for the main part, to that time.

The era of great battles on the plains of Europe was over. But a time of political unrest in the interior of the various European States set in; this unrest reached its culminating point in the explosions of 1848. Such unrest was a source of particular satisfaction to England, for it weakened and disorganised all her Continental rivals.

Down to the time of the Crimean war (1855), the Eastern question remained veiled in considerable obscurity; England, Russia, Turkey, France, and Austria-Hungary played a curious and very complicated game of political and diplomatic chess. This game was still further complicated when Mehmed Ali appeared on the scene, and marched on Constantinople. It is impossible, within the limits of the present work, to dwell on those events. We must content ourselves with describing, in general terms, the part played by

England. The latter did not wish to see any of the Continental Powers in possession of Constantinople; and she also wished to prevent by all means an alliance between the Porte and any of the Powers. It was from these two considerations that English policy derived its principle of the "maintenance and independence" of Turkey. That policy, on the other hand, aimed at drawing Turkey as much as possible into the meshes of Great Britain's net; in this way Turkey could be conveniently played off against France or Russia, as the occasion required it. Being herself an insular Power, England needed the services of a Continental Power in all Eastern matters. According as time or circumstances dictated, Austria-Hungary or France was selected for this honor; but Russia was not disdained either if the occasion required it. During the period of Mehmed Ali's insurrection, English policy had three distinct aims in view: firstly, to prevent Mehmed Ali from capturing Constantinople; secondly, to prevent the development—desired by France—of intimate relations between him and the French Government; thirdly, to prevent him concluding an alliance with the Sultan, and thus strengthening the Porte. Great Britain's anxiety concerning France was not unfounded; for the French had turned their eyes towards Egypt. In all these lengthy quarrels, the decisive word was spoken by the all-powerful British navy. The old English principle, according to which every opportunity should be seized upon in order to destroy all foreign fleets—whether the latter were peaceful or hostile at the moment of destruction did not matter: this principle proved extremely valuable. Its utility (from the English point of view) had been manifested in 1807, at the moment of the theft of the Danish fleet. Thus did it come about that, at the instigation of Great Britain, the Turkish fleet was destroyed "by mistake" at Navarino. An allied Anglo-Franco-Russian fleet sailed in 1824 to Navarino, where the Turkish fleet lay. An agreement had been made whereby negotiations should take place with the Turks, and it had further been resolved by the allied commanders not to open fire unless the Turks did so. Suddenly a shot was fired, and it has never yet been ascertained on which side; but the English declared that it was the Turks who had fired it. The result was the destruction, or rather the massacre, of the wholly unprepared Turkish fleet. The English Admiral had already received his instructions from London, but in the British Parliament all this was, of course, denied. The English Prime Minister even gave utterance to the memorable words: "The destruction of the Turkish fleet was an untoward event." But "unfortunately" could things not be changed! Mehmed Ali's future fleet had been partly annihilated, partly captured by the English, whose ships, in turn, occupied with success the ports and harbors of Syria.

Both at that time and also in later years, the limits of sea power have been very clearly demonstrated in the Near East. England was in a position, thanks to her navy, first of all to protect and coddle the new-born Kingdom of Greece, and subsequently to humiliate and bully it. This changeable attitude was kept up until King Otho's successor, who was related to the English royal family, ascended the Greek throne. It was, again, her navy which permitted England to assume the rôle of "guardian" of growing Italy; and this navy it was, also, which caused the cunning policy of Napoleon III in the Mediterranean to collapse. But the aspect of things changed, as soon as the center of gravity of the Eastern conflict was removed to the Continent. It then became necessary for England to buy a "continental sword"; with the Power employed as such, England co-operated cheerfully until there was no further need of the former's services. The tool was then cast aside.

Russia was, during the first half of the nineteenth century, fully aware of this fact, and pursued her policy of expansion accordingly. Her object, as usual, was Constantinople and the Dardanelles. Her ambitions led to the Crimean War, in which France and Italy were the auxiliaries of Great Britain. The Crimean War was badly managed, and the English performances at sea were likewise lamentable; especially those of the Baltic squadron, to which was entrusted the task of attacking the Russian coasts and of destroying the Russian fleet. But the consequences of the Treaty of Paris proved that England alone had profited by the war. The antagonism between France and Russia—antagonism which had been increased by the conflict—was destined to cost France dear not long afterwards. On the other hand, England had obtained, in conjunction with France, the neutralisation of the Black Sea and the closure of the Dardanelles and Bosphorus. Nothing shows better who was the real winner in this war, than the fact that the French were particularly anxious to conclude peace rapidly; whereas England, by raising perpetually new questions during the negotiations in Paris, and by seeking up till the last moment to create complications, endeavored to prevent peace being concluded.

Prussia had taken no part in the Crimean War, despite the strongest English pressure, despite threats and insults. Her abstention was one of the first great political acts of Bismarck. The latter recognised that it would have been folly for Prussia to show hostility to Russia in those days.

The Prussian-German Customs' Union was, from the beginning, a thorn in the side of the English. Its foundation had been combatted by all possible means, and the efforts directed towards the protection of German industry had been denounced as an "unfriendly act" against England. Nothing was left undone, either by the British Government or by its accredited and unaccredited agents, in order to fight and to intrigue against the proposed Union in every German State. There are certainly few things which can be more legitimately included in the category of a country's "internal affairs," than the settlement of their mutual economic interests by the German States. But England had, in the most cunning manner, arranged, at the Congress of Vienna, for Germany to become an object of economic exploitation, and had imagined that matters would always remain thus. Knowing its own unassailable position, the British Government overdid things. Especially did the elevated English duties on wood and corn, which were arbitrarily modified in London, place German production and shipping in an ever more untenable situation; on the other hand, British industry continued to throttle German production, and to deprive the latter of its rightful profits. When Lord Palmerston was at last ready to give way, and offered, amongst other things, a reduction of the English duties on wood, it was too late and there remained nothing for the noble lord to do but to submit and accept the *fait accompli*.

Another event had, during the thirties, spoilt Great Britain's game: namely, the separation of Holland and Belgium, whose reunion England had been foremost in bringing about at Vienna. Belgium had separated herself from her Northern neighbor, for that which cannot be united cannot be held together. English policy recognised this fact, and quickly decided to "make as good a job of it" as possible. The European neutralisation of Belgium was the consequence. As the historian Louis Blanc wrote: "England kept the diplomatic scepter in her hand, and exploited the Belgian revolution to her own advantage." Belgium's neutrality was directed solely against France, because England was convinced that the French would seize the first opportunity of bringing Belgium under their influence. In view of the state of affairs existing at the present moment, it is interesting to observe that the Treaty of Neutrality was concluded exclusively on account of France, whose ambitions it was meant to restrain. England hoped, by inducing the European Powers to participate, under her own leadership, in the guarantee of Belgian neutrality, to reserve for herself the possibility of organising, if need be, another coalition against France. De facto the newly created Kingdom of Belgium was entirely under British influence; it became England's advanced post on the Continent, the outer line of her fortifications. And no one in Europe could prevent this.

During that period France was the "enemy"; and a remarkable parallel can be traced between the events which then occurred, and those which have taken place within the last quarter of a century—events which we will consider later on. In the fifties Great Britain succeeded in utilising her "enemy" against Russia in the Crimean War; she induced France to sacrifice her troops and warships, and to weaken herself generally, for the sake of British interests. At the same time, both during that war and previously to it, Great Britain was everywhere busy working against France—and especially in Egypt. Shortly after the war she enticed France into the Mexican adventure, and then, as usual, retired from the scene herself, as soon as the stone had been set rolling. Great Britain's object was to create difficulties between France and the United States, by bringing the former into conflict with the Monroe Doctrine; she further wished to weaken France in Mexico, and to discredit Napoleon in France. The plan succeeded brilliantly. Within recent times it was intended to use the German Empire against Russia in the same way as France was used sixty years ago.

Great Britain found it impossible, during the sixth decade of the last century, to stem the flowing tide of German unity. The reasons for this were, firstly, the superiority of Bismarck's diplomacy and political genius; secondly, his fearless determination; and, thirdly, the fact that purely Continental interests were at stake. During that curious period of European political development, Bismarck was the only statesman whose will was strong and unbending, and who knew exactly what he wanted.

The far-sightedness of English statesmen had recognised, early already in the sixties, that the power of Napoleon was on the wane. They observed with satisfaction that the Emperor of the French was constantly obliged to seek the creation of new "stage effects," in order to maintain his prestige, and to consolidate the throne for his successor. At the same time Napoleon's policy never ceased to be a cause of uneasiness for England; and the Suez Canal enterprise roused John Bull to violent indignation. How could a Continental Power dare to construct a canal joining up two seas, and thereby render a great British ocean highway valueless? We know how Disraeli's business talents subsequently succeeded in transforming the peril into a profit, after the canal had been built. The spendthrift Khedive, Ismael Pasha, was overburdened with debts; Disraeli purchased all his Suez Canal shares, obtained later on possession of others, and thus placed the canal under the virtual control of England. Ever since the great insurrection of the Seapoys in 1857, the British Government had worked uninterruptedly to bind India to the Empire, and to organise her defence. The Suez Canal was a first-class instrument for this purpose. The Anglo-French rivalry in Egypt continued, but the English influence there increased steadily. In the rest of the world, during the nineteenth century, England did and took what she wanted. If any territory, in any region whatsoever, appealed to the taste of some wandering English merchant or politician, he simply hoisted the British flag, and the matter was settled. The territory was henceforth British.

About the end of the sixties it became perfectly evident to English statesmen, that Germany, under Bismarck's guidance, was advancing rapidly towards unification. At the eleventh hour British diplomacy tried hard to prevent this unification from taking place. In London the thread was spun of an elaborate intrigue, which aimed at persuading the North German Union and France to come to an understanding regarding a reduction of armaments. The proposal met with considerable approbation in France, whereupon the latter became suddenly England's "friend." Weakness, aimlessness, discord, were becoming ever more and more visible in France; and these sorts of things have always been calculated to earn England's friendship. But the London Cabinet had no success in Berlin with its proposal. Bismarck politely declined, and did not budge an inch. The English took similar steps in South Germany, where they did not content themselves with proposing a reduction of armaments, but also argued most persuasively that the union of the Southern German States with the Northern ones would be a crime against humanity which Europe could not possibly tolerate. The Southern States, further, would be doomed to certain perdition, i. e. be crushed under the Prussian boot.

When the great war with France broke out, English public opinion was at first considerably affected by Bismarck's revelations, to the effect that France had endeavored, before the war, to obtain his consent to the French annexation of Belgium. Soon afterwards English opinion became pronouncedly favorable to France, and remained so. Munitions were sold to the French, and everything else that the latter wanted; the bombardment of Paris was bitterly criticised; the annexation of Alsace-Lorraine called forth a storm of curses. Gladstone intended protesting against it. But all this anti-German feeling remained confined within very modest limits, for England had other and very grave anxieties. The Russian Government declared itself released from the obligations imposed by the Treaty of Paris, and it found herein the firm support of Bismarck. France was momentarily crushed, and Austria-Hungary was not capable of resisting Russia and Germany by herself. England thus found herself isolated, and was compelled to sacrifice an important article of the Treaty of Paris—namely, the neutralisation of the Black Sea. This was decided upon in a conference held in London. In 1871 England found herself powerless in regard to affairs on the Continent. There was "nothing to be done," and with that practical sense which is so developed in the Englishman, the English Press did not shrink from an exhibition of grovelling hypocrisy. Towards the end of 1870 an essay appeared in the Times, of which the conclusion furnishes interesting reading to-day:

"I think that Bismarck will take as much of Alsace and Lorraine as he wishes, and that this is all the better for him, all the better for us, all the better for the whole world—except France, and in course of time better for her also. By means of his quiet and splendid measures, Herr von Bismarck intends realising one great object: the welfare of Germany and of the whole world. May the broadminded, peaceful, intelligent, and earnest German nation then attain to unity, may Germany become the Queen of the Continent, instead of the light-hearted, ambitious, quarrelsome, and far too irritable France!"

But such sentiments as those expressed here, were not, in London, of long duration.

In the course of the following years, England did not succeed in carrying out her traditional policy of a coalition organised against the Continental Power which happened for the time being to be the strongest: namely, Germany. England's antagonism to Russia increased continually. Austria-Hungary was absorbed by internal quarrels, and remained weak; France had to recover from the war, and found herself to be politically dependent on Berlin. British statesmanship deemed it, consequently, advisable to be on good terms with Bismarck, whose support England required for her policy in the Mediterranean. In the latter sea England had every interest in opposing French expansion. Italy was used for the purpose; and the center of gravity of the English fleet was likewise transferred to the Mediterranean. The French fleet had remained intact during the war, and constituted an important factor of the balance of power. France and England soon came into conflict: in Egypt, in the rest of North Africa, in the Far East. Italy varied her position during the seventies, she was not well led, she was unable to follow up an independent and consistent policy, and she lacked initiative. Not until 1881, when France snapped up Tunis under her very nose, did Italy join the Austro-German alliance. England herself drifted, precisely on account of her Mediterranean interests, towards the Triple Alliance; and her relations with the latter became more and more friendly at the beginning of the ninth decade.

During the seventies Anglo-Russian relations grew very strained, and a rupture between the two countries appeared imminent whilst the Russo-Turkish war was in progress. The British fleet was anchored before the Dardanelles. At Russia's demand, the Congress of Berlin met under the presidency of Bismarck; the Preliminary Peace of San Stefano was revised very much to Russia's disadvantage; and England emerged triumphant from the diplomatic struggle. Not only had she forced Russia to retreat, and strengthened the Balkan position of Austria-Hungary; but she had seized Cyprus and concluded a treaty with Turkey. It was at this time that British diplomacy, under Disraeli's leadership, succeeded in sowing the first seeds of discord between Russia and Germany; those seeds were destined to bring forth fruit. That Russian distrust of Germany set in, which never disappeared again, but which, on the contrary, only grew stronger. Nevertheless did Bismarck succeed, in 1884, in concluding a Neutrality Agreement between Germany, Austria-Hungary, and Russia. In England, the successful policy of the German Chancellor was praised; but, behind the scenes, everything possible was done with a view to checkmating and nullifying it. The triple entente between Germany, Austria-Hungary, and Russia soon came to an end as a result of the tension between Austria-Hungary and Russia in the Balkans; in its stead Bismarck concluded the celebrated Reinsurance Treaty with Russia. This treaty was very distasteful to Great Britain, for it prevented the latter from playing off Germany against Russia. Russia's policy of expansion in Asia was a source of growing anxiety to England, who was used, in such cases, to rely on the assistance of a Continental Power. Such assistance could not now be obtained on account of Bismarck's alliances; on the other hand, France was also an antagonist of England's, and sought to effect a rapprochement with Russia—albeit, until the end of the eighties, in vain.

England did not feel at all well in her "splendid isolation"; for the first time was she obliged to recognise the fact that, without a Continental "servant," her influence in Europe was but small, as soon as a strong will manifested itself here. To add to this, the Germans initiated a colonial policy which sorely vexed Her Britannic Majesty's Ministers. That policy, it is true, was a very modest one; but it made the English uneasy, just as the new German steamship lines did. But Bismarck pursued his aims unflinchingly, and informed the London Cabinet that Germany would be glad to march hand-in-hand with Great Britain in all matters of colonial policy and colonial conquests. If England did not desire this, then Germany would come to an understanding with France.

The greatest pain and annoyance that Bismarck ever caused our English friends was in 1879, when he proceeded to establish a protective tariff for German industry. The protection of European markets against English industry is, according to English conceptions, the most hostile and outrageous act which a nation can possibly commit against the Chosen People. If England had found herself at that time in a more advantageous political position and if Bismarck had not been there, it is probable that Germany's conversion to Protectionism would have had much more important effects on Anglo-German relations than it did. We need only remember the Anglo-French wars about a hundred years before, the origin of which is to be traced chiefly to disputes arising from similar causes.

CHAPTER VIII
ANGLO-GERMAN FRIENDSHIP AND ESTRANGEMENT AFTER BISMARCK'S DEPARTURE
1890–1895

It is well known that the anxiety felt concerning alleged warlike intentions of Russia, and also the belief in such intentions, played a part in the events which led up to the fall of Prince Bismarck. It was greatly to England's interest that this belief should prevail in the governing circles of the German Empire; for as soon as it existed, and became strong enough for political consequences to result from it, the end of the Reinsurance Treaty with Russia must necessarily be in sight. And this is what did in fact happen. When Caprivi took over the Chancellorship after Bismarck's fall, he had nothing more urgent to do than to refuse Russia's offer to renew the Reinsurance Treaty, with a haste which Bismarck qualified in the Hamburger Nachrichten as altogether excessive. No one could have been more delighted than Great Britain! The experienced statesmen on the banks of the Thames, who were so intimately acquainted with all the laws which govern the grouping of European Powers, knew immediately that the abandonment of the treaty in question—especially in the form adopted—must mean the end of the former confidential relations between Germany and Russia. Great Britain knew, as well as Bismarck did, that a partly written Agreement had already existed for some years between France and Russia. Who could tell whether the entente between Russia and Germany, on the one hand, and France and Russia, on the other, might not lead to a Franco-German-Russian Alliance? For Great Britain, no spectre more uncanny than that of a co-operation—to say nothing of a real union—between the leading Continental Powers could possibly be conjured up. As long as Bismarck was there, English statesmen had found no opportunity of driving a wedge in between Russia and Germany. But in 1890 they succeeded with ease in doing so. The natural consequence of all this was to hasten and to consolidate the intimacy between France and Russia. Henceforth neither the Court nor the Government in St. Petersburg offered the same determined resistance to the Pan-Slav agitation as they had formerly done. Bismarck had been able to say in days gone by that all Pan-Slav intrigues had but the weight of a feather by comparison with the authority with the Czar. All that was now at an end. By means of the Reinsurance Treaty Russia had insured herself against the attacks and the pressure of her worst enemy, which was Great Britain. Ever since the seventies, an Anglo-Russian war had been one of the probabilities of European politics; for the points at which the two nations came into hostile contact were constantly increasing in size and number, alike in the Balkans and in Asia. It was therefore of the greatest importance for Russia that she should have, in case of war, a friendly neutral Germany on her Western frontier. The entente with Germany gave Russia the further assurance that, owing to the Austro-German alliance, Austria-Hungary would not allow herself to be induced by Great Britain to take part in a war against the Empire of the Czars.

It will be seen therefore that, in the complicated situation created by the Reinsurance Treaty, Great Britain was at a distinct disadvantage. As long as the Treaty existed, Great Britain had not a single Continental Power at her disposal; and this appeared all the more dangerous to her on account of the growing colonial expansion of France, and in view of Russian expansion in the Near East and in Central Asia. England sought, under these circumstances, to effect a close rapprochement with Germany. The Morning Post, the organ of the English Prime Minister, Lord Salisbury, wrote at the beginning of the reign of the Emperor William II.: "Neither England nor Germany are thinking of a war; but it must appear every day more evident to both countries that, if war should indeed be forced upon them, they will have to stand or fall together. No paper alliance is necessary for this." It was the time when the friendship of Germany was eagerly desired, and when the Reinsurance policy was at its last gasp. Great Britain's friendship seemed at first tolerable enough; but the situation grew dangerous in the very moment when, after the non-renewal of the Reinsurance Treaty, the Franco-Russian alliance commenced to manifest pronounced anti-German proclivities.

Caprivi was deeply convinced of the necessity of an intimate friendship between Germany and England. He wished, consciously and intentionally, to place the German Empire under British guardianship, in all matters of maritime, commercial, and colonial policy. After the wooing of Germany by England had succeeded in its object of separating the former from Russia, England's tone towards her newly-acquired "friend" suddenly changed. The aim had been realised, the possibility of a great Continental coalition had been suppressed, and no further wooing was necessary—seeing that Germany now appeared in a certain degree isolated. Already in 1891, a representative of the British Government took the opportunity of declaring that, in the event of a Franco-German war, England's national interests would have first and foremost to be considered. Not without reason was public expression then given to such a self-evident truth; in spite of all "friendship," in spite of "standing and falling together," the British Government deemed it useful to drive home an important truth: namely, that if war were to break out between France and Germany, England would take sides either for or against the latter—according to the circumstances. Already in 1890 England had signed a Colonial Agreement with France; and since that date she had more than once given it to be understood that she was perfectly willing to develop more intimate relations with the Republic. To Turkey's demand that Egypt should, at long last, be evacuated, Lord Salisbury replied with the delightful euphemism: "We wish first of all to complete our work there." About the same time, the friendly relations of Germany and the Ottoman Empire commenced; and the initial steps towards building the future Bagdad railroad were taken.

During the years of unhealthy Anglo-German "friendship," England considered Germany as a servant who owed her obedience. In 1890 the Zanzibar Agreement was signed, and in 1893 a second Agreement was concluded; both were drawn up entirely from the standpoint of English interests. When Germany shortly afterwards entered into a Colonial Agreement with France—in which, be it said, the former once more got the worst part of the bargain,—England resented this; her resentment increased when Germany and France both protested, a year later, against a convention concluded by England with the Congo State in violation of international treaties. About the same time the Prince of Wales undertook a journey to Russia; the British Government seized the opportunity of settling temporarily its quarrel with St. Petersburg concerning Central Asia; and the English press was able to talk ironically about Germany's isolation.

In 1894 the German Government sent two warships to Delagoa Bay, as a demonstration against English intrigues which threatened the independence of the Boer Republics. At that time the Boer newspaper Volks Stem wrote: "Up till now the Germans have let us settle our disputes with England by ourselves; but at last it would seem that Berlin has recognised the erroneousness of this policy. In the name of the Boer people we tender our thanks to the German nation." This was, in truth, an historical moment; for ever since then English statesmen turned their attention to two problems: firstly, the prevention of the development of closer relations between Germany and the South African Republics; secondly, the destruction of the independence of the latter. We must once more remind our readers of the fact that England knew perfectly well that Germany was no longer backed up by Russia; and that Germany was, consequently, isolated in all questions of world politics. The Triple Alliance played no part in these; just as little as Germany herself, did the Triple Alliance possess a naval force which England needed to pay even the slightest attention to. Therefore did the British Government draw the noose ever tighter round the neck of the South African Republics, which it was determined to destroy by hook or by crook. Cecil Rhodes began his activity, created new territories for England all around the Boer States, and thus isolated the latter. In England, the enmity against Germany had increased so rapidly, that already in the summer of 1895, when the German Emperor visited the Queen of England, the English Government press received him with marked hostility. The London Standard published a much-noticed series of articles which, under the pretext of welcoming the Emperor, criticised him with bitter irony.

Ever since the combined efforts of England and Austria-Hungary had checked Russia's expansion in the Balkans, the Government of St. Petersburg had pursued systematically and energetically its "forward" policy in the Far East. England felt her own interests in this region to be more and more menaced; and already a quarter of a century ago her experienced statesmen had recognised Japan as the Power capable of rendering invaluable service in the struggle against Russia. At the beginning of the nineties, England and Japan concluded a treaty of commerce and friendship. During their war with China in 1894–95, the Japanese were financed by English bankers. This war had the result of separating Corea from China—Corea, which was the goal of Russian policy. China was also compelled to surrender the peninsula of Liaotung, with Port Arthur, to Japan. Here, again, England stood behind Japan, for the former knew that Russia had designs on Port Arthur. In view of the Japanese demands, Russia, Germany, and France decided to intervene together. The German view was that if Japan were to establish herself on the Asiatic Continent, this would mean her definite ascendancy over China; from an economic standpoint, Japan "would stand like a sentry at the entrance to the highways leading into China, and would command them." In addition to this, Germany had concluded a secret convention with Russia, the result of which was later on the leasing of the territory of Kiaotchow.

Japan was forced to give way to the pressure of the three European Powers, and to surrender the peninsula of Liaotung. Russia, on the other hand, was conceded the right of constructing a branch of the Transsiberian railroad to Port Arthur; a few years later, the latter was given over to her on lease. Germany took Kiaotchow, and England Weihaiwei. At the time of the war between Japan and China, Germany was not yet regarded by England as an end, but only as a means: a means against Russia. England was unable to check Russia's expansion in the Far East; for Russia was in the happy position of possessing an uninterrupted and direct line of communications by land with the Pacific Ocean. The sea power of Great Britain was impotent as regards the Transsiberian railroad. The still rudimentary sea power of Japan had shown itself to be as yet too weak to be used as a British battering-ram against Russian Imperialism in those regions. And it was natural and inevitable that France should be on the side of her Russian ally. There thus remained only the German Empire, as the one Power capable, in the eyes of England, of stemming Russia's expansion in the Far East. But Germany adopted a precisely contrary attitude and went over to the other side, for the reasons above indicated. Therefore were the English filled with indignation against the German Emperor, on account of what they termed his "liking for political experiments."

In South Africa, about the same time, the last act but one of the great drama took place. Dr. Jameson and his band of filibusters made their disgraceful raid on the Transvaal. The Boers captured them, and the German Emperor despatched his famous telegram to President Krüger. The English ought to have approved of this telegram, if the conscience of the Government and the nation had been, with regard to the Raid, as pure as was maintained. But such was not the case; and there ensued an appalling outburst of fury against the Germans in general, and the Emperor in particular.

The British Government proceeded immediately to get its fleet ready; a part of this was sent to Delagoa Bay, and the rest was held in readiness in the home waters, just as if a war with Germany were contemplated. We do not know the diplomatic communications which took place at the time between Berlin and London. The German Government declared semi-officially that it was not true that any apologies had been offered on its behalf in London. And both the Government and the press confirmed the absolute unity of Kaiser and people.

An English newspaper, on the occasion of this tension between the two countries, asked ironically how Germany represented to herself a war with Great Britain. It was evident that, unless Germany worked systematically in harmony with other Continental Powers, she could not possibly act, in any overseas question, in opposition to the British Government. If she did, her failure was a foregone conclusion; for there was no German navy. Joseph Chamberlain, who was then English Colonial Secretary, said at the time with characteristic frankness, it was the object of every British Government to maintain England's position as predominant Power in South Africa; the aim of the Government was the union of all the South African States under the protection of the British flag. The English Colonial Secretary thus declared, in so many words, that England would not rest until the Boer Republics had been deprived of their independence by one means or another: the old traditional British policy of brigandage! The main cause of England's greed was the existence of diamonds and gold in the territory of the South African Republics; then came subsequently the fear that the economic and colonial expansion of Germany might dry up the English waters in South Africa altogether. In conformity with English traditions, these real motives were concealed behind a cloak of pompous and hypocritical phrases about civilisation, culture, etc. After the Krüger telegram the British Government had, by means of its naval demonstrations, put (symbolically) to the German Government the question of power; and having done this, it considered *ipso facto* the South African policy of Germany as knocked on the head. Such was, indeed, the case. Bereft of a fleet, Germany could not pursue, with regard to England, any policy which raised the fatal question of power.

CHAPTER IX
"AND IF THOU WILT NOT BE MY SERVANT...."
FROM 1895 TILL THE ENTENTE CORDIALE

The prosperity of German industry, of German trade, of German shipping, and the development of German capital, began, about the middle of the nineties, to attract the attention of an ever-growing number of persons in Great Britain. Such "attention" on the part of the English is, as we know, invariably tainted by animosity. From all oversea countries arrived reports from British consuls and commercial agents, telling of German competition in the foreign markets. Everywhere was the German merchant to be found, who was unusually active, who spoke all languages, and who endeavored most skilfully to find out the wants and wishes of the native population, to which wants the manufactured goods were subsequently adapted. The immense growth of German industry had been rendered possible by the Protectionist policy inaugurated by Bismarck in 1879. The protection of those national forces which demanded to be developed, against foreign competition—especially against British industry,—was an imperative necessity. Bismarck had not let himself be caught in the English net so carefully spread for Continental birds—i. e. by the "doctrine" of the blessing of free trade for German industry. As soon as it was protected, German industry revealed a strength hitherto unsuspected; it could now thrive; and the more it could thrive, the more could it expand; and thus was it ever more and more in a position to satisfy all requirements as to quality. After a very short time, the English jeers about German industrial products, which were scoffed at as being "cheap and nasty," produced no effect. Then came England's great and irremedial mistake. In order to protect English buyers against worthless German products, the British Government decided that all manufactured goods imported into Great Britain, Ireland, and the Colonies, should in future be marked: "Made in Germany." Thus did England, the champion of the magnificent ideal of Free Trade, decide. As is well known, the plan failed, and the German products, thanks to their good quality and their cheapness, obtained instead an unlooked-for success; for the English buyer got into the habit of asking for German, instead of English, goods. This failure, with the involuntary comedy and the still more involuntary English irony attached to it, produced its repercussion in the whole world, and became an universal and well-deserved advertisement for German industry. The culminating point of the German triumph was reached, when the German liner Kaiser Wilhelm der Grosse entered the port of Southampton bearing the inscription "Made in Germany" in large letters.

The English were not yet uneasy. The tremendous start which it had, enabled British industry to dominate its rival in all markets. The immense difference between the means of production and distribution, and especially between the capital, at the disposal of either country, was well known. This fact alone was sufficient to prevent any uneasiness cropping up. Lack of German capital, and an extreme and lasting tension of German credit, on the one hand; immense English capital on the other: such was the position of affairs towards the close of the last century.

But England is in the habit of carefully observing even the first rudimentary beginnings of everything calculated to damage the monopoly, which Providence has granted her in the markets of this world. In 1896 the former Prime Minister, Lord Rosebery, declared in a public meeting that he attributed the disturbance of the friendly relations between England and Germany not only to the Transvaal question, but above all to the fact that Germany was beginning to catch up England in the economic race. He himself was quite surprised by the technical and commercial progress achieved by the Germans; German competition in these spheres was a danger of the future. Germany possessed the most complete system of technical education, and was therefore the most dangerous rival of England; in fact, she even menaced British trade in India and Egypt. The same politician said later: "We are threatened by a terrible adversary, who wears us out as surely as the sea wears out the unprotected parts of a coast. I refer to Germany."

Lord Rosebery was quite right. What he termed a disturbance of the friendly relations between Germany and England—namely, the outburst of mob fury in the latter country after the German Emperor's telegram to President Krüger—was due only in part to the South African complications. In fact, these certainly furnished the lesser motive, for Great Britain, being all-powerful at sea, had nothing to fear in the future from Germany in South Africa. The South African question was settled. But German commercial competition, and the development of German industry, were quite different matters. They could be suppressed neither by a *quod non* of the British Government, nor by a clatter of swords. The principal motive of English unrest resided in the feeling, partly conscious and partly unconscious, that German trade had risen from humble origins to an astonishing height of prosperity by its own unaided efforts, and in spite of the most difficult conditions. In the course of our pilgrimage through the centuries which tell of the development of British piracy, we have seen that it is by no means the superior capacity or the originality of the English people which have permitted them to obtain possession of the markets of the world. An exceptionally favorable geographical position; the ability to inflict in the most cunning and unscrupulous manner damage on other nations, which were either exploited if possible by their best forces being drawn by England into her own service, or which, if this was impossible, were paralysed in such a way that they destroyed themselves: such have been the factors of the development of British wealth and power. The incurable madness of the Continental Powers, which perpetually tore each other to pieces and exhausted their resources for the greater glory of the British grocer, did the rest. But never did the superior productivity, the superior intelligence, and the honest work, of the English, have a share in the building up of England's monopoly. Germany before the Thirty Years' War stood, in respect of such qualities, on a far higher level than England, as did also Italy at the time of the Renaissance, Holland in the seventeenth century, and France in the days of Colbert and of Napoleon I. And now, after the long interval that had elapsed since the War of Liberation, during which the monopoly of industry and trade had appeared to the English as if it were given them by Providence—after all these years, there suddenly arose the new German Empire. The latter was, it is true, as yet without many resources; but it proved itself a hard-working and talented competitor. Was it not inevitable that the noble British blood should boil? How could the German nation, which up till then had been poor and despised, dare to compete with British industry, not only in the German but even in the English market—nay, even in the world market?

Statistics showed that, during the period 1873–1896, the number of German vessels had increased sixfold, and their tonnage more than tenfold. The German passenger service was unrivalled in the world; the North Sea fishing trade was formerly exclusively in English hands, and the German fishing fleet in those waters had now been increased twelvefold since 1873. The oversea shipping trade of Germany had increased by more than 100%, whereas that of England had only increased by 35%—a clear proof that German trade was proceeding with giant strides to liberate itself from the English intermediary. Precisely this last-mentioned phenomenon caused unusual pain and annoyance to the "world's carrier," for it was equivalent to a severe blow in the face. The German consulates in oversea countries increased in number every year. Every year also did the total trade of Germany grow, and of this trade much more than half was done with oversea countries. The amount of money invested in the latter, and the number of shipping lines and of shipbuilding yards, likewise augmented every year. Everywhere the English saw growing strength, and the spirit of enterprise, and perseverance, and skill—everywhere an indomitable resolution to produce only the best of everything. In 1896 the German flag was, for the first time, to be seen in Hamburg in superior numbers to the English. It was, on the one hand, a legitimate triumph for the Germans, and a sure sign that matters were progressing steadily; on the other hand, it brought home to them once more all the misery of the years gone by. Not until twenty-six years after the foundation of the new German Empire had the numerical superiority of British ships in the greatest German harbor been done away with! Up till then trade with German ports had been carried on principally under the British flag, and via British ports. Such was the fruit yielded by the "great harvest" reaped by England at the time of the war with Napoleon, when England, albeit at peace with the State of Hamburg, blockaded the mouth of the Elbe, and seized Hamburgian ships wherever she could find them. Hamburg now took peaceful revenge, and thereby prodigiously excited the wrath of the benefactor of mankind at the other side of the North Sea.

In order that this period of Anglo-German relations be rightly understood, it is impossible to insist too often on one cardinal fact: namely, the absence of a German navy right up till the commencement of the twentieth century. A few warships, it is true, existed, but these were small, and the majority of them were badly built. England rightly had no respect for such a fleet. As for Germany's world policy, and the tendencies revealed by the latter, the British Government judged it solely in the light of a factor of possible alliances and groupings of Powers. In other words, British statesmen were first and foremost concerned about the question: with which Powers will Germany seek to effect a rapprochement, in order to obtain support for the aims pursued by her world policy? This was very natural, seeing that every co-operation of Germany with another Power appeared to the Government of His Britannic Majesty as a menace and a danger. This Government believed also to have found here the key to a further conundrum—namely, how may German trade competition be guided into paths where its danger to England shall be reduced to a minimum? The best solution to both questions appeared to the London Cabinet to lie in a rapprochement between England and Germany. It was known in London that Germany would create no difficulties in South Africa; and this sufficed for the moment. When Russia took Port Arthur, and Germany acquired Kiaotchow, whilst England followed suit with Weihaiwei, the British Government considered it to be of great importance that Berlin should be informed of the former's firm intention "not to call in question any of Germany's rights or interests in Shantung." The British Government was aware that Port Arthur had been for some years the goal of Russian policy in the Far East, and that the leasing of Kiaotchow to Germany could not possibly constitute a danger to English interests for a very long time to come. Or did other intentions prevail already in those days? We do not know. In any case must Port Arthur in Russian hands have appeared to British statesmen as distinctly dangerous; for it was the symbol of Russian expansion in the Far East, and of an Imperialist policy which could only be pursued at the expense of the Chinese Empire. The acquisition of Weihaiwei was in the nature of a counter-move directed against Russia, and not against Germany. Mr. Arthur Balfour, the future Prime Minister, in the course of a speech made at the time, gave expression to the anxiety felt by the Government concerning the perilous surprises which the development of events might entail for the future of China. The Russian danger in the Far East had become immense, for Russia's expansion threatened the freedom of the Chinese market, which Great Britain had long since attributed to herself, and which she had sought to prepare by all the means in her power. A steady increase of the Russian fleet proceeded simultaneously with the Russian advance on the Continent. Every new warship was despatched to the Far East; Port Arthur became a naval port and a fortress, whereas Dalny, in the neighborhood, was made into a trading port.

Thus it was the Russian danger which induced the British Government to seek a rapprochement with Germany. We may resume England's policy at that time in a sentence: if possible, let us make use of Germany against Russia. The former, and Austria-Hungary with her, can by means of pressure—and, if necessary, by war—in Europe, loosen Russia's hold on the Chinese Empire, and indirectly check the Russian advance in the Far East. This calculation was, in itself a perfectly sound one. There is no doubt that an European war, which would have relieved England of her anxieties in the Far East, would at that time have been very welcome to the British Government.

Prince Bülow kept his hands free, and the British wooing did not have the success which the late Joseph Chamberlain wished for; but the London Cabinet continued to hope that it would eventually attain its end. In the last years of the old century events succeeded each other rapidly. The Hispano-American war broke out, and Spain lost the greater part of her remaining colonial possessions. All the other Powers remained neutral. England, however, despite her friendship with Germany in the Far East, seized the opportunity to endeavor to sow in the United States the seeds of distrust against Germany. British diplomacy observed with irritation and anxiety the victorious campaign of the Americans, but did not venture to give public expression to its feelings. It contented itself with an effort to prevent the armed intervention of the United States in Cuba, by means of a joint action of the neutral Powers. Germany refused her co-operation; and British diplomacy at once proceeded to put matters in such a light that it should appear as if Germany, and not England, had proposed taking this step. The British cable companies did everything they could—and that was a great deal—to prevent all possibility of a German-American rapprochement ever being realised.

The same year 1898 witnessed an event which was destined to become a most important turning-point in British modern history: namely, the so-called Fashoda affair. As is well known, this "incident" was created by a French expedition under the leadership of Colonel (then Captain) Marchand, which, setting out from the French Congo, had reached Fashoda, in the territory of the Upper Nile. The English considered any French advance towards the last-named region as constituting a grave danger for their own position in Egypt. Lord Kitchener, who had just won the battle of Omdurman, protested against the hoisting of the French flag at Fashoda. Captain Marchand declined to give way, and notified his Government of the incident. A great tension of Franco-British relations immediately followed, and England's language became very menacing. The Under-Secretary of State for Foreign Affairs in London, Mr. (now Lord) Curzon, had declared, a year before, at the time when Captain Marchand had just begun his expedition, that if the latter should enter a territory "in which our rights have already long been recognised, this would not only be an unexpected act, but the French Government must well know that it would be an unfriendly one, and considered as such in England." Such language was already clear enough; but much stronger language was resorted to when the event actually took place. The Naval Reserves were called in, the fleet was held ready, and the English Ministers, as is customary in all such cases, made speeches of a most menacing character. Their argument was the following: England claims to rule over all territories having formerly belonged to Egypt; she does so "on behalf of Egypt," which country has, at the cost of the heaviest sacrifices, been saved from anarchy and ruin. The claim, as will be seen, was a very elastic one. It amounted to this: wherever, within the limits of the African Continent, England chose to declare that a territory had once belonged to Egypt, such a territory was transferred by Divine right to the Chosen People.

France was not prepared to defy Great Britain. In the spring of 1899 the latter concluded an Agreement with the French Government, by means of which she obtained all she wanted: namely, the recognition of her uncontested right to rule in all territories which the Egypt of yore had ever claimed, or ever could claim. England did not, of course, demand this in her own name, but in that of the "independent Egyptian State." Had France not given way, it would seem that England intended taking Tunis, with the naval port (then in construction) of Bizerta.

"The disgrace of Fashoda" was, from that time on, a popular phrase in France, and the Germans believed that they were now but a short distance removed from a Franco-German understanding. It was, however, a great mistake. The leading men in France were convinced that the Fashoda "incident" had quite another meaning. The French colonial plans, which had found their expression in the Marchand expedition, had definitely failed. Other colonial problems in Africa were still open. The French fleet would, in the future, be just as little in a position successfully to defy the British fleet as it had been in 1898. No effective help on sea could be expected from Russia, for the center of gravity of Russia's policy and maritime power lay in the Far East. It is true that France could maintain a respectable fleet in the Mediterranean, and thus keep up a certain equilibrium there. Her fleet was sufficient to prevent France being eliminated from any settlement of

Mediterranean questions. But the French statesmen were of opinion that France was henceforth too weak to continue the old historical struggle with England on the seas and beyond them. Subsequent reflection confirmed their first impression. Since July, 1898, M. Delcassé was Minister for Foreign Affairs, and M. Paul Cambon was French Ambassador in London, where he is still to-day. M. Cambon, a leading political personality and a diplomatist of the first order, saw that the moment had come for paving the way to an understanding with England. It is reported that M. Delcassé, on taking office, likewise said that he hoped not to leave the Ministry on the Quai d'Orsay until he had laid the foundations of a lasting entente with the latter Power. The French press could wax indignant about the disgrace of Fashoda, it could demand peremptorily an increase of the navy, and threaten the hereditary foe,—this war of words left Great Britain wholly indifferent. The statesmen in London knew full well that a great turning-point in history had been reached; and they were content to wait quietly until the fruit should ripen.

The Fashoda incident had, therefore, an entirely different meaning to the one which is still generally to-day attributed to it. It was not in spite of Fashoda that six years later the Franco-English entente was concluded, which has since developed into an alliance—but as a result of Fashoda! Without Fashoda there would have been no *Entente Cordiale*, no alliance! The old historical world-struggle between France and England reached its definite end with the Fashoda incident. Even after 1870 it was still conceivable that France might endeavor, in conjunction with Continental Powers, to resume the ancient struggle—especially in view of the burning questions arising out of the conflicting colonial aspirations of the two countries in Africa. The Fashoda incident put an end to all this. The efforts made during the preceding twenty years by statesmen on both sides of the water, in view of arriving at an understanding between Paris and London, had been temporarily frustrated by Bismarck. But now, after the tree had been vigorously shaken at Fashoda, the fruit fell spontaneously. We may recall, in this connection, the words spoken by the French Ambassador in London in the days of the Krüger telegram: "France has but one enemy," etc.

After Fashoda the political situation in the Mediterranean was suddenly changed. It was no accident that France and Italy should, about the same time, have effected a rapprochement after long years of estrangement, and that they should have signed a colonial agreement. Crispi had inaugurated Italy's ambitious colonial policy, and had induced the Italian nation to make immense efforts in order to become a great Mediterranean Power. The defeat at Adua signified the end of this era; instead of the ambitious foreign policy which aimed at placing Italy ahead of France in the Mediterranean, a new period now set in, characterised by timidity and excessive economy in matters of national defence. The party which denounced Italy's adhesion to the

Triple Alliance as the cause of ruinously expensive armaments constantly increased. We now know that English influence stood behind it, that English counsel and English intrigue prepared and organised the unfortunate Abyssinian adventure, partly in order to give British troops a pretext for intervening themselves, partly because England had no use for a powerful Italy in the Mediterranean—much less so, in fact, since the weakness of France had become palpable. Formerly, when France was stronger, England had done all she could to embitter the quarrel between the two Latin nations; but now it was the reverse. Thus it was that England, in 1898, bestowed her blessing on the Franco-Italian rapprochement, by the mouth of Admiral Rawson, Commander-in-Chief of the British squadron, which was then visiting Genoa. England likewise succeeded, on the same occasion, in loosening the ropes that bound Italy to the Triple Alliance; Italy veered round in the direction of France and England, attracted as she was by the advantages offered her in North Africa by these two Powers. England was, from now on, no longer the Power whose fleet served to back up the Triple Alliance (which possessed no fleet) in the Mediterranean, where England had guaranteed the maintenance of the *status quo* against France. This policy of England's was no longer necessary, for France no longer dreamt of "kicking against the English pricks." Not the least of the causes which, in former days, induced Italy to join the Triple Alliance, was the former's rivalry with France.

The reasons for the destruction of the Boer Republics were typically English. These Republics grew and prospered, and became stronger in every way; it was only natural that they should aspire to complete independence in their relations with other Powers, and that they should not consider themselves as bound by a forged treaty limiting their rights in this respect, and which had been forced on them by England some fifteen years previously. The British Government, and especially Chamberlain, understood that a normal and natural evolution was here in progress, and that it could not be stopped. The only means of doing so remained the destruction of the independence of the Boer Republics.

During the Boer War the anti-foreign movement known as the Boxer War, broke out in China. All the European Powers sent troops to the Far East, and a numerous international fleet was anchored in Chinese waters. The *leitmotiv* of British policy at that moment was furnished by the necessity of checking Russian expansion in the Chinese Empire and in Corea. Already during the Boxer troubles, England and Japan worked together on the most intimate terms; on the other hand, British diplomacy endeavored to play off Germany against Russia in China, and was very dissatisfied when it observed that the Germans intended acting in the Far East on their own account—chiefly in view of obtaining new openings for German trade. England was likewise displeased with the relatively strong fleet which Germany had despatched to the Far East; she had, on the other hand, the consolation of seeing the German fleet in home waters reduced to two battleships.

The only reasonable policy which Germany could possibly pursue during the Boer War, was one of absolute neutrality. When Russia attempted to take advantage of the situation, and to induce Germany to take part in a movement against England, Prince Bülow put an end to all further negotiations by proposing, as a condition of the intervention of the European Powers, that they should agree to recognise the validity of the territorial *status quo* on the Continent. In this way, France would have had to accept the Treaty of Frankfort, and the idea was consequently abandoned. Russia was the only Power which could, at that time, by an advance towards the Indian frontier, have fought with success against Great Britain.

Thus England remained undisturbed, and with her freedom of action unimpaired. Alone the business instinct of the United States skilfully took advantage of the situation, and a new treaty concerning the future Panama Canal was concluded. The sovereignty of the United States over the Canal was thereby assured, and the latter withdrawn for ever from British control.

During the Boer War, Lord Salisbury and Joseph Chamberlain continued their efforts to bring about an understanding with Germany. It was proposed to form, in conjunction with the United States, a German-Anglo-Saxon Alliance. Chamberlain declared that no far-sighted British statesman could wish to see England permanently isolated from the Continent. Her quarrels with Germany had been mere trifles, and could not obscure the fact that, German and English interests were, to a large extent, parallel; and that the most natural alliance for England was an alliance with the German Empire. Some weeks later Prince Bülow replied that the German Government likewise desired to come to an understanding, but that this would only be possible on the basis of absolute equality and mutual respect. Germany consequently must desire all the more sincerely that no incidents should crop up, susceptible of creating difficulties between the two countries. Such an "incident" was the confiscation, by the English, of German mail steamers during the South African war.

Finally an agreement was made, on the basis of the *status quo* and of the open door in China. We would recall that Japan was also a party to this agreement. The London Cabinet thought that it had thereby caught the German Empire in the meshes of the English net, seeing that Germany had bound herself over to protest in company with Great Britain and Japan against the Russian advance in the Far East—for that advance menaced the *status quo* and the open door alike. There followed the negotiations with Russia regarding the evacuation of Manchuria by the Russian troops. (The latter had occupied Manchuria during the Boxer War.) Russia promised the evacuation, but did not fulfil her promise. But Prince Bülow declared in the Reichstag that the Anglo-German-Japanese Agreement did not concern Manchuria. The fate of the latter province was wholly immaterial to Germany.

The attitude of Germany in the Manchurian question was the cause of the definite abandonment, by Great Britain, of her attempts at wooing. It is probable that the idea of a rapprochement with France originated in London simultaneously with the end of the Anglo-German flirt. The ground, as we have seen, was already prepared. France was only waiting, she had submitted herself to the inevitable, and her clever diplomatists were skilfully and noiselessly working with a view to removing the last obstacles.

The Anglo-Japanese Alliance was but the logical consequence of the situation which had been created in the Far East by the war between China and Japan, by the intervention of the European Continental Powers in 1895, and by the expansion of Russia. There can be no doubt that the British statesmen had long been at work. They had for a long time intended drawing Japan, as the strongest adversary of Russia, over to their side. On the other hand, the hope of avenging "the disgrace of Shimonoseki" had operated powerfully among the Japanese nation. England, with the one definite aim of checking Russian expansion before her, had assisted the Japanese Government in every way—with money, credit, political and naval advice. With the help of the Chinese war indemnity and of British loans, Japan, between 1895 and 1904, built up a small but excellent fleet, and organized her army according to the German pattern—whereby she was actively seconded by German officers, who were engaged as instructors. These officers laid, during years of peace, the basis of the Japanese victories, which were due first and foremost to German military science. The German army manœuvres also played their part, for they were frequently visited by studious and energetic Japanese officers. Thus did German diplomacy, on the one hand, and the German army, on the other, take diametrically opposite sides: namely, for Russia, and against her. Truly a deplorable spectacle!

The way in which the Russo-Japanese War was prepared, begun, and carried out, furnishes another typical example of British methods. England did not need to have recourse, in the case of Japan, to arguments—for Japan was already convinced. England only needed to pour oil on the fire, to add to her ally's strength where this was necessary, to take the political and diplomatic reins into her own hands—and then, when war had broken out, to point with unmistakable clearness to her all-powerful fleet which ruled the seas. Under these circumstances, who else could venture to say a word? Japan fought England's battles on sea and on land. The Russian fleet was annihilated at Tsushima and in the harbor of Port Arthur; the Russian armies were driven with terrible loss from Liaotung and Manchuria. Port Arthur fell into the hands of the Japanese. The satisfaction in London would certainly have been greater if the Japanese triumph had not been so overwhelming. England wished the Russian fleet to be entirely destroyed, but she would also liked to have seen three-quarters of the Japanese fleet at the bottom of the sea. Instead of that Japan became, thanks to her navy, the predominant Power in the Far East. This solution was not, from the English point of view, an ideal one; but it was not an unprofitable one either—or at any rate any disadvantages it might have, did not seem likely to manifest themselves for a very long time to come. It was England who, cleverly screened behind the United States, prevented Japan from obtaining a war indemnity in Portsmouth. In this way did the two Anglo-Saxon nations inflict far greater damage on Japan, than was ever inflicted by the intervention of the Continental Powers in 1895. Japan's army and navy have thereby suffered considerably in their development up till the present day; the Japanese finances have ever since been in a critical condition; and the population as a whole has been reduced to a state of poverty resulting from overtaxation, such as no country has ever witnessed after a victorious war. About the same time, England caused the Alliance between herself and her impoverished friend to be consolidated, and the duties resulting from it for either Power to be extended. On the whole, the danger in the Far East had been suppressed; Japan had been bound to Great Britain and rendered economically dependent on the latter. Japan's resources were exhausted, and she had been placed in the impossibility of recovering her strength for many years to come. England sought, at the same time, to widen as much as possible the gulf, already then perceptible, between America and Japan. It was in England's interest that the gulf in question should not be bridged over—but, on the other hand, the quarrel must not be allowed to lead to war. The London Cabinet has had, nevertheless, considerable difficulty at times in preventing war from breaking out.

Russia, on the other hand, had been immensely weakened by her defeats and by the revolution; and for a long time she could undertake nothing. But England was desirous of obtaining still more. Even as Fashoda had proved the beginning of the Anglo-French entente; so also were Tsushima and Mukden destined to form the bridge between St. Petersburg and London.

CHAPTER X
DELENDA GERMANIA
THE BEGINNING OF KING EDWARD'S REIGN

When King Edward ascended the throne of England, he at once took decisive steps to bring the Boer War to an end. He likewise without delay set about drawing the consequences which arose from the Fashoda incident, and from the Anglo-French colonial agreement of 1899. He had evidently first of all carefully prepared the way, in the course of discussions with French and English diplomatists. In May 1903 King Edward went to Paris, and soon afterwards President Loubet, accompanied by M. Delcassé, returned the visit in London. In the autumn of the same year a treaty of arbitration was concluded between the two countries; and on April 8th 1904, the celebrated Anglo-French convention was published. This convention formed the basis of the *Entente Cordiale*, which has existed since 1905. The understanding between France and England was an event of the highest importance in the history of the world, for it marked the first great step taken on the road leading up to the war of 1914, which England so carefully organised and prepared and set in motion.

The convention of 1904 put an end, once and for all, to all the colonial quarrels between England and France. The work of liquidation, begun in 1899, was finished five years later. Bismarck had understood, by a skilful handling of African colonial problems, how to prevent a rapprochement between the two Western Powers; especially had he understood the art of keeping the Egyptian question—that chief bone of contention—alive. Fourteen years after Bismarck's departure, the last seeds of dissension sowed by this policy of his were dug up and destroyed. With the exception of a few unimportant reservations, France renounced all her claims to intervene in Egyptian matters. England promised, partly in public, and partly in secret, agreements, to assist her French friends in obtaining Morocco. There is no need to go here into details. The most important point was the fact of the union of the two Western Powers. Two months only had passed since the outbreak of the Russo-Japanese War, when the Anglo-French Convention was published; England hereby showed the world that not only Japan, but also an European Power, was at her disposal—and this European Power was none other than the Ally of Japan's adversary.

British statesmanship had not succeeded in reducing the German Empire to the position of England's humble servant. Consequently was Germany henceforth England's enemy; with the support, and sometimes under the leadership, of King Edward, the British Government was from this time forth to have recourse to all those methods of which experience had shown the value, and which we have encountered in the course of our historical survey in the present book. Already some years before the Anglo-French Convention, English influence could be observed at work in shaping the relations between France and Germany. French distrust of Germany, due to the alleged desire of conquest and oppression of the German Government, constantly increased; the co-operation of French and English in the Mediterranean, with the aim of detaching Italy from the Triple Alliance, grew ever more and more active. Since 1903 the English hand was busy all over the political chessboard—especially in the Near East. Public opinion in Great Britain had already attained to such a pitch of hostility that, in the autumn of 1904, after Russia's Baltic fleet had sailed for the Far East, important English newspapers publicly declared that the moment had now come for placing Germany in front of the alternative of either ceasing the construction of her fleet, or of having the latter destroyed by British warships. In Germany such articles were not taken seriously; it was said that they were the work of loud-mouthed jingoes, and without any importance. As a matter of fact, such an ultimatum to Germany was, at that time, under serious consideration in London.

The British Government had well chosen the time for the Anglo-French Convention. While Japan was fighting England's battles against Russia in the Far East, King Edward and his statesmen extended the hand of friendship to France—the ally of the same Russia whom Japan was fighting by England's order. France found herself before that date in an uncomfortable position. She could not help her ally, and she did not even venture to send warships in any considerable number to the Far East. On the one hand, France feared for her East Asiatic colonial possessions; on the other, she feared Russia's displeasure at the absence of all assistance from her ally. In addition to this, there was the risk of France finding herself isolated with regard to Germany. Under these circumstances England appeared as a savior, and as a prop to lean on. At the same time French diplomacy, always very skilful, seized the opportunity in order to prepare the way for a future rapprochement between Russia and England. The idea of such a rapprochement had already been entertained by Sir Edward Grey in 1903. From the beginning, Sir Edward Grey had been an opponent of Chamberlain's policy of alliances. Thus did the efforts of French diplomacy meet with a favorable reception in London; to British statesmen a rapprochement with Russia now appeared just as desirable as the rapprochement with France had appeared after Fashoda. A weakened Russia was a very welcome friend indeed.

CHAPTER XI
EDWARD VII PREPARES THE HUMILIATION AND DESTRUCTION OF GERMANY
1905–1908

The first European crisis engendered by the new British policy broke out in 1905. On account of her geographical situation on the shores of the Atlantic and the Mediterranean, with her Northern coast bordering the Straits of Gibraltar, Morocco is a country of much importance; England wished her now obedient vassal France to take possession of it. Spain, it is true, was to receive a strip of territory as hinterland to Ceuta, while Tangier was to remain "international." It was forbidden, in the interests of England, to fortify the coast near the Straits of Gibraltar. With these reservations Morocco was handed over by Great Britain to France. Germany was intentionally ignored, and the convention of 1904 was not even brought officially to the knowledge of the German Government. The latter waited a whole year, but when the French Government commenced taking steps with a view to placing Morocco under its protectorate, Germany protested; the final result of her protest was the resignation of M. Delcassé. The policy of this statesman had been to refuse systematically all German demands, even at the risk of war. He was convinced that Germany would retreat the moment she knew that Great Britain had decided to stand by France and to back up the latter energetically. The attitude of the Premier, M. Maurice Rouvier, and the declaration made by the Ministers of War and Marine to the effect that France was unprepared for war, brought about the departure of M. Delcassé quicker than England had expected it. The "inner" history of the crisis of 1905 is not yet fully known; but the course taken by events shows sufficiently clearly that the London Cabinet subsequently took the reins into its own hands. The attitude of the French Government, which had at first been conciliatory, changed within a very short time, and became either dilatory or hostile; and when the German Government made the great mistake of proposing an international conference to settle the Moroccan question, Germany found herself alone in front of an overwhelming hostile majority. Here is not the place to discuss the aims which our Moroccan policy set itself in those days. The basis of Prince Bülow's policy was invariably the open door, the principles of which he and his successors always consistently upheld. The German Government was further of opinion that war should not be waged on account of Morocco, unless a question of national honor were involved. Prince Bülow believed this to be no longer the case after the departure of M. Delcassé. On the other hand, the public and secret agreements between France and England aimed at creating a condition of affairs, the inevitable result of which could not but be the destruction alike of the open door, of the integrity of Morocco, and of the sovereignty of the

Sultan. To speak, under these circumstances, of the open door, was to maintain a fiction in which no one could believe. The fact that the German Government consistently kept up this fiction, necessarily awakened in England and France the impression that Germany only wished to "save her face" in the eyes of the world, and that she would on no account wage war. This was certainly the weakest spot in the armor of German diplomacy, at a moment when the latter was face to face with very resolute adversaries. For Great Britain was resolved to prove to the world that she and her new ally France were in absolute opposition to the German Empire; she wished further to prove that a war could only be prevented by a German retreat. All the demands of the German representatives at the Algeciras Conference were rejected, and not a single Power was to be found to back up Germany energetically. German's isolation was so complete, that she was thankful to Austria-Hungary when the latter's representatives declared themselves ready, in one particularly knotty question, to build a bridge over which the Germans could effect an honorable retreat. The Algeciras Act, a very voluminous document, was from beginning to end a complete farce. Those who knew the conditions did not for a moment doubt that it could never be put into practice. The secret agreements between France and England were alone sufficient to deprive the Act of all value. As a matter of fact it was never enforced, and France never allowed herself for one minute to be influenced—much less bound—by it. To a certain extent did the Conference keep up appearances, as far as Germany was concerned; but in reality the whole thing was a failure from beginning to end. The new European policy of England had stood its first test. In 1905 it was clear to all the nations of Europe, with the exception of the Germans, that henceforth international politics would be dominated by the Anglo-German rivalry.

Before and during the Algeciras Conference, preparations were going on in view of an Anglo-Russian understanding. Russia had been vanquished in the Far East, and British diplomacy drew the logical conclusion from her defeat. The idea found active and enthusiastic supporters in France, who were also anxious to create a Triple Alliance directed against Germany. A number of opportunities for working together were furnished by the Algeciras Conference. On the other hand, Germany experienced a disagreeable surprise on seeing Russia, who had apparently entirely forgotten the invaluable services rendered her by Germany in her hour of need, combat all the latter's demands at the Conference. Italy had already entered previously to the Conference into certain obligations towards France and England; she had, in return, been granted by these Powers a right of priority in Tripoli. The Italians were also to be found at Algeciras among Germany's adversaries; the same was the case with nearly all the smaller European States, and with the United States of America. This was a phenomenon, the importance of which completely overshadowed that of the Moroccan question taken by itself. With extraordinary skill, rapidity, and energy, England's statesmen had understood how suddenly to represent the German Empire as the disturber of European peace, as a danger to France, and as jealous of Great Britain.

A short time before England herself had been quite isolated, and she had only recently emerged from out of the grave crisis of the Boer War, and from out of the not less grave crisis in the Far East; and yet, already in 1905, King Edward and his advisers had been able to come to an understanding with France and Russia. They had further succeeded in loosening the ties which bound Italy to the Triple Alliance; and, quite apart from the question of a participation of Italy in a war, they had managed to induce her to place, at the Algeciras Conference, her diplomacy at the service of Germany's adversaries. Up till a few years previously, Germany had been on excellent terms with Spain. England spoke a few words behind the scenes, Spain was promised a piece of Morocco and was henceforth to be counted likewise among Germany's opponents. British diplomacy had succeeded, during the Venezuela affair, in creating in the United States such intense bitterness against Germany, that the Americans, albeit the Morocco question did not concern them in the least, could not wax sufficiently indignant at the spectacle of German "illegalities" and "attempts to disturb the peace of the world."

In the following year, 1906, the understanding between England and Russia was effectively concluded. In 1907 it was sealed by the agreement concerning Persia and Central Asia. The co-operation of the two Powers in Oriental questions immediately commenced. The Russian defeats at Tsushima and Mukden had produced the consequences desired by British statesmen. Incapable henceforth of continuing her policy of expansion in the Far East, bereft of nearly her entire fleet, weakened at home by the revolution, Russia now judged it to her interest to be on friendly terms with the very Power to whose systematic intrigues and icy-cold calculations all the misfortunes of the Empire of the Czars were due. The Anglo-Russian Convention put an end to the anxiety hitherto felt in London concerning the possibility of a Russian advance on India by way of Central Asia. Persia was divided into spheres of interest, between which a neutral sphere was created, and in this way peace was also assured here. England did, in fact, relinquish many of her hopes and ambitions in Persia, for the sake of arriving at an understanding—deemed to be of priceless value—with Russia. During the years which followed the war with Japan, British and French diplomacy were equally active in their efforts to turn Russia's attention towards the Balkans and Constantinople. The object was to create friction and dissension between Russia and Germany, and between Russia and Austria-Hungary. England intended that here also Russia should fight her battles for her—this time in conjunction with the Balkan peoples—just as she had fought them in the Far East.

King Edward and his Ministers attached particular importance to the friendship of the smaller States, and England's "wooing" was done skilfully and systematically. Frequent journeys consolidated the personal ties of friendship uniting rulers and statesmen, and England was always able to promise either real or apparent advantages. With Greece and Italy the old relations of guardian to ward were resumed, as also with Spain. King Edward succeeded in placing a British Princess on the Spanish throne. The reconstruction of the Spanish fleet was entrusted to English builders, and a Spanish loan was floated in London in order to cover expenses.

England and France concluded with Spain a so-called Status Quo Agreement concerning the Mediterranean, whereas nothing is known in regard to the conventions signed about the same time with Italy. It is, however, certain that they were likewise directed against Germany. In the North of Europe, British policy had been able to register a great success: namely, the division of the hitherto united Scandinavian monarchy into the two kingdoms of Sweden and Norway. These two large countries, united under Swedish leadership, lived on friendly terms with the German Empire. This could not be allowed. With the help of all the means at her disposal for use in such cases, England set to work; the result being that the old Norwegian jealousy was rekindled, and a separation became inevitable. A Danish Prince with an English wife ascended the Norwegian throne, and ever since then Norway has stood under English influence. Everything was done with a view to inducing Denmark to come over to England's side. In 1905 a British fleet visited Esbjerg, and afterwards passed through the Skagerrack and Kattegat. It was during the time of the political tension caused by the Morocco difficulty, and the world had just learnt, through the so-called revelations of M. Delcassé, the plans of the British Government with regard to a landing in Jutland. The Danish royal family at that time would doubtless have been inclined to draw the sword in a war against Germany; but not the Danish nation—with the exception of some fanatics. At any rate, when the English fleet paid its visit to Esbjerg, a representative of the Danish Government took the opportunity of declaring that the latter's programme consisted in a single word: neutrality. He was thereby referring alike to the English crimes of 1800 and 1807, and to the war of 1864 with its consequences. We would observe, by the way, that Denmark was already in 1905 of great strategical importance to the English, on account of the question of the passage of the fleet, in time of war, through the Sound and the Great Belt. Ever since 1900 the English press had been full of articles concerning the passage through these waters in time of war; and every effort was made to persuade the Danish nation that, in the event of such a war, its place must be at the side of England. The journey of the English fleet through the Skagerrack and the Kattegat to the Baltic in 1905, was undertaken for reasons which cast a very clear light on the thoughts and intentions of British statesmen. During the Moroccan crisis the British Admiralty announced, quite suddenly, that the North Sea Squadron would go to the Baltic for the purpose of practising there. In the press comments on the matter, we find the view expressed that the Germans considered the Baltic as a closed sea belonging to Germany, and that they considered the growing strength of their navy to give them the right to claim it. But England wished to show the whole world that she did not recognise such a claim, and that she was determined to let the British fleet perform its practises in every sea which it should please the Admiralty to select. So far the press. The voyage of the British fleet was therefore nothing else but a threat—and a wholly unjustifiable one. Neither the German Government nor the German people had ever entertained so foolish a thought as that of regarding the Baltic as a closed sea. In our days a sea can only be shut from outside; and to close the Baltic in times of peace to the fleet of another nation would be a silly and meaningless act, even if the German navy were capable of enforcing such an order. The journey of the British fleet, which was extended so as to include visits to a number of German Baltic ports, was, as we have said, nothing but a well calculated and demonstrative threat. It was destined to prove to all the Northern States that, if it pleased the British fleet to penetrate into the Baltic and to visit German ports there, nothing could stop it; the German navy would be but an insignificant hindrance in time of war. Therefore, o ye Northern States, do not venture to stand by Germany, or it will be the worse for you!

In 1905 and 1906 England concluded definite agreements with Belgium in case an European war should break out. The agreements were completed by other conventions between France and Belgium, and between France and England. Belgium, as is well known, was a neutral State. Already at this time England knew that, in the event of a war between France and Germany, the former, relying on the strength of the line of fortresses on the Franco-German frontier, would march through Belgium with a view to invading Prussia. But England had a poor opinion of French organisation, and of the French army as a whole, and judged it necessary to take steps in the matter herself. In the military conventions with Belgium, an Anglo-Franco-Belgian plan of campaign against Germany was worked out in all its details. England desired to land an expeditionary corps, and wished under all circumstances to make Antwerp a basis of supplies: all this has been proved by documentary evidence already published. When we analyse these events it appears incontestable that, quite apart from purely military considerations, England intended, by means of her co-operation with Belgium, to lay hands on Antwerp. English policy, as usual, was playing a double game. According to the way in which events shaped themselves, the British expeditionary troops could either march directly against Germany, or they could remain on Belgian soil, and occupy Antwerp or other towns on the coast. In this way, Belgium would have developed from a simple outer fortification into England's Continental basis of operations, and England would have opened, by virtue of her own power, the mouth of the Scheldt at Holland's expense. Belgium would have become a second Portugal, and England would have had the free use of all her harbors, etc. The military conventions drawn up by England with Belgium in 1905–06 pursued very ambitious aims—political, naval, and military. It was at this time that Belgium forfeited her neutrality and became the obedient ally of England, and also of England's chief servant France.

The British Government endeavored to go still farther, and to form a great anti-German union of the neutral States. With this aim in view, every effort was made in order to bring about an alliance between Holland and Belgium. The plan was frustrated by Holland's refusal. Both in peace and war the Dutch Government has maintained the same strict and honorable neutrality, however difficult it may have been at times to persist in such an attitude. By the formation of a Union of the Neutral States, Great Britain would have created a union of vassals, which would have appeared on the scene as soon as the war against Germany had broken out. The existence of such a plan is likewise proved by documentary evidence, discovered since the outbreak of hostilities. All this goes to show how extensive were the preparations made, in view either of holding the German Empire in check by inspiring it with fear—or else, if need be, of waging the war so that it must result in the total destruction of Germany alike as a trading Power, a political Continental Power, and a maritime Power.

CHAPTER XII
THE INCENDIARY AT WORK
THE CAMPAIGN AGAINST THE GERMAN NAVY

No one in England felt in the least uneasy about the German navy. Nothing but contempt was entertained for the "Emperor's toy." It was compared to a crow, which had adorned itself with a parrot's feathers; and everywhere proofs were adduced of the superiority of the English fleet, alike as regards quantity and quality. Such were the views held in well-informed circles. But none the less was the German Navy, even when still very small, held up as a terrible instrument of war. Already in the first years of the new century the following argument was frequently to be met with in England, whence it was transmitted to the whole world: Germany, and more especially the German Emperor, is planning to attack and destroy the British fleet, after which it is intended to send across the North Sea an army, that shall land on the holy coasts of Great Britain and reduce the liberty-loving Britons to slavery. It will suffice if we mention these absurd stories; it is not necessary to refute them here in detail, but we must lay stress on the fact that they were never believed for a moment by a single serious politician or naval expert in Great Britain. Such stories were invented and circulated, simply because they were considered to be politically useful. In this way the German Empire could be conveniently represented as the Power which was carefully preparing for an aggressive war, and which was bent on disturbing the peace of Europe. Being past masters in the art of organising such campaigns of slander, the English knew that the most idiotic lie will be believed, if only it be repeated often enough and in the proper tone of virtuous indignation. And this is what did, in fact, happen. The real motives underlying British policy since 1902 all find their expression in the motto: *Germaniam esse delendam*; and these motives were skilfully concealed behind the humbug relating to the German navy. It is evident that the British Government did not desire such motives, dictated by mere vulgar jealousy of German industry and German maritime trade, to be recognised as the real basis of its policy. Therefore it was sought to conceal, wherever possible, these motives behind a veil. The German navy proved an admirable "veil." Whoever takes the trouble to compare the number and the size of the warships then existing in either country, will at once admit this.

After King Edward had succeeded, by means of the entente cordiale with France, in bringing about the great change of front in England's foreign policy; and whilst he was consistently and perseveringly pursuing his work along the lines laid down; the British Admiralty, on the other hand, commenced taking steps with a view to modifying the conditions of national defence, so as to adapt them to the requirements of the new political situation. A thorough reorganisation of the Navy began in 1905; not only was the fleet's readiness for war largely increased, but above all was its distribution over the various seas completely rearranged. As soon as France had become England's faithful vassal, it was no longer necessary that the Mediterranean should remain the center of gravity of British naval policy. This center of gravity was now transferred to the North Sea. The Russian fleet had been destroyed at Tsushima; the strong British squadron hitherto maintained in Chinese waters was henceforth superfluous, and was consequently recalled to the English coast. A considerable number of cruisers, which had been stationed in different parts of the world, were likewise ordered home. In short, in the course of a few years, nearly the whole of the British fleet was concentrated in front of the eastern shores of Great Britain. Ample measures had been taken in Great Britain itself in view of this concentration. New harbors and dockyards were constructed, new naval stations called into being, all along the North Sea-coast; it was something entirely new in British history, for the British naval front had always extended from the South East to the South West—along the shores of the Channel in the direction of the Atlantic. Of course, this truly epoch-making redistribution of the British fleet had only one object: namely, the safeguarding of the British Isles. The entire fleet must be concentrated in order to prevent its destruction by the German navy, and in order to defend Great Britain against invasion. A movement in favor of compulsory service in the army accompanied the reorganisation and redistribution of the navy. The movement in question was organised by Lord Roberts; the fleet, it was urged, could not be absolutely relied upon to prevent a German landing—and such landings were planned, and would take place in a moment when none expected them. Lord Roberts commenced his agitation in 1905, and threw the whole weight of his authority—which in England was great—into the balance. In Germany his "invasion speeches" were taken seriously, and people really thought that this cunning old fox believed what he said. Today, after documentary proofs of the Anglo-Belgian negotiations have been brought to light, these credulous Germans will perhaps understand that Lord Roberts's propaganda was a well-organised "fake"—seeing that Lord Roberts could not possibly tell the truth as to his real motives. In reality, he and his supporters did undoubtedly wish the army to be increased by means of compulsory service in view of an invasion. But the invasion of which they were thinking was a British invasion of Belgium! The author of the present book has defended this thesis for the last eight years; the documents found in Brussels, and the operations of the war themselves, confirm it entirely. The projected invasion was not the least of the causes which prompted the British Admiralty to concentrate almost the entire fleet in the North Sea; for that fleet was necessary, if troops were to be transported safely to Belgium. Lord Roberts did not succeed with his programme of compulsory service; but British Ministers of War, and notably the "pro-German idealist" Haldane, were able none the less, with the already existing means at their disposal, to prepare the invasion of Belgium in such a way as to excite general surprise—especially in Germany.

King Edward and his Ministers wished, if possible, to prevent a further increase of the German navy; they wished to save expenses for their own country, and to be able—as was later on frequently said in England—to undertake without any risk the destruction of every European fleet. Solely with this aim in view did a new epoch in the annals of British warship-building begin—in the year 1905. This epoch is known as the "Dreadnought era," from the name of the first battleship of that type. The leading men in Germany, however, realised the importance of the hour. They understood that it was not only the future of the German navy as such which was at stake, but that the question was wider still: namely, the question of the possibility, for Germany, to pursue henceforth, whether in Europe or beyond the seas, a policy which should not be dependent on England's good will or displeasure. It is possible that the German Reichstag, and a large section of German public opinion, did not see so far ahead; but it was sufficient that they understood the welfare of the navy to be involved. The result was, that Germany at once proceeded, on the basis of the already existing Naval Law, to construct Dreadnoughts; and that the work of widening-up and deepening the canal between the Baltic and the North Sea, as well as all other canals, harbors, etc., was immediately begun. The naval and political decisions taken, in Germany, in 1905 and 1906, were of the highest importance; and their consequences have made themselves—and will continue to make themselves—felt far beyond naval circles. England's attempt to "outdo" Germany by the invention of Dreadnoughts, had failed. For some years still it was believed, in England, that the Germans would not overcome the technical difficulties entailed by the construction of the new type of warship; but this illusion was destroyed in 1908.

If we consider the above-discussed attempt to "outbuild" the German navy in the light of England's general policy, we shall see that the former was entirely consistent with all British historical traditions. The German Empire had never done England any harm, it pursued no hostile aims, it had not intrigued against British interests, it had not endeavored to engineer an anti-British coalition. The German Empire had, on the contrary, invariably acted in pure self-defence, whether from a political or from an economic point of view. History has never known a policy more peaceful than that pursued by German statesmen. The German fleet could not possibly, either in its conception or in its development, constitute a danger for Great Britain. None the less Germany was a great Continental Power, her trade and industry flourished, she claimed the right of protecting her national production, she tried to build herself a fleet: therefore must she be destroyed. How monstrous the English lies about the "German danger on the sea" were, is proved—but this is merely *en passant*—by the fact that in August 1914, after fifteen years' activity, the German fleet, viewed as a whole, was not even half as strong as the British.

CHAPTER XIII
KING EDWARD'S UNSUCCESSFUL ATTEMPT TO SET THE NEAR EAST ABLAZE
THE BOSNIAN CRISIS

The policy of Great Britain in the Near East has undergone frequent and apparently unaccountable modifications. At times England supported the Sultan, at others she was against him; she would one day preach the doctrine of the sanctity and inviolability of the Dardanelles treaties, and the next day she would herself send a fleet into the Dardanelles. The same Power which was full of enthusiasm for the integrity of the Ottoman Empire would later on, amidst plentiful groans and sighs, steal a piece of that Empire for itself. With a stentorian voice which could be heard over the whole world, the British Government denounced the "atrocities" in Armenia or Macedonia; and at the very same moment emissaries sent out from London, and notably the famous "Balkan Committee," were busy, in Armenia or Macedonia or elsewhere, stirring up trouble and creating disturbances which caused the very "atrocities" in question to be perpetrated. We see England working hand-in-hand alternately with Russia and with Austria-Hungary. Where is the thread connecting the whole of British policy in the Near East during the last twenty-five years?

Sultan Abdul Hamid was, for British statesmen, the incorporation of everything bad and detestable. They pretended to feel disgusted even when pronouncing his name. He had failed to carry out the reforms which he promised after the Russo-Turkish war; he was an "oppressor," he allowed "atrocities" to be committed in Armenia and Macedonia. The English even declared, with an expression of unutterable disgust, that Abdul Hamid occasionally caused "undesirable" persons to be done away with. In reality, this intensely virtuous indignation was due chiefly to the knowledge that Abdul Hamid was an extremely clever politician and diplomatist, and to the fact that he would not consent to renounce his claims to Egypt. Abdul Hamid had the most disagreeable habit of raising the Egyptian question from time to time, and precisely at the very moment when it was least convenient for the British Government. He had the further extremely disagreeable habit of keeping up, with the utmost skill, a game of ball between the Great Powers, in which the ball was never definitely caught and always rebounded. The Sultan used to play off the one against the other, and in his able hands Turkey's chronic "sickness" became a valuable diplomatic asset. England's aim was, of course, to bring the Turkish Empire entirely under British influence, and then to deal with its various component parts according as circumstances required. The first object of British statesmen was to combat Russia's efforts to obtain possession of Constantinople and the Dardanelles.

In order to attain this object, it was necessary to treat the Porte alternately as a friend and as an adversary. Albeit, mistress of the oceans and of the Mediterranean, Great Britain was, until the conclusion of the *Entente Cordiale*, seriously uneasy about Russia's desire to obtain, in conjunction with France, a solution—if need be by force of arms—of the Dardanelles question.

Shortly after the accession of the Emperor William II to the throne, an entirely new factor in the politics of the Near East arose. The first journey of the German Emperor to Constantinople attracted the attention of Europe. This journey was displeasing to Russia, and consequently gave satisfaction to England. The German Government declared that its friendship with Turkey aimed exclusively at the obtention of economic advantages, and that it entertained no political ambitions whatsoever. The first railroad concessions to German companies in Turkey followed, and formed the beginning of the future great Bagdad undertaking. Ever since that first visit of the German Emperor to Constantinople, the friendship between Germany and Turkey has continued almost without interruption. The explanation is to be found in the simple fact that the German Empire is the only Power which did not wish to increase its influence or its possessions at the expense of the sovereignty of the Sultan, of the financial and economic strength of the Ottoman Empire, and of the latter's territorial integrity.

It is evident that England's traditional policy in the Near East could not but make her regard the friendly and confidential relations between Germany and Turkey with the greatest dissatisfaction. It was, in the first place, an insult to England that the new Power Germany should venture to enter the ranks of the nations which were interested in Turkey. England was all the more uneasy, because her statesmen clearly recognised that Germany's policy of maintaining and strengthening Turkey was not a mere pretext, but honest truth. England did not want a strong Turkey, and did not dream of tolerating one. The stronger Turkey became, the less could Egypt be relied on—and the more intimate, also, must become the connection between Constantinople and the Islamitic world. Precisely this connection appeared to England, who rules over so many millions of Mussulmans, as a grave danger for her in India, Central Asia, and Africa. And we know that British statesmen are extraordinarily far-sighted in all matters where danger of any sort is to be detected.

In addition to all this there remained the main source, as usual, of British anxiety: the market. It was disgraceful and unheard-of, an insult and an unfriendly act, that German industry should dare to penetrate ever more and more into the Ottoman Empire. British industry had already a hard struggle to maintain itself here against the French and the Austro-Hungarians. And now the Germans came on the scene! England's uneasiness was increased by the projected German railroads; and ever since the beginning of the new century she did all she could during ten years, in conjunction with France and Russia, to hinder the construction of the Bagdad line. The Germans encountered here a fundamental principle of British policy; and all such principles, as we have often shown, have their roots in British trade. England has invariably been the most decided adversary of all great railroad undertakings—in so far as they were not in British hands or under British control. British statesmen have always been well aware of the fact that every important railroad which is withdrawn from British control, diminishes British sea power and British maritime trade. The mistress of the seas controlled all the waterways of the world, which she could shut or open as she pleased. The "world's carrier" had at her disposal a trading fleet vastly superior to all others, an immense quantity of harbors owned by herself, to say nothing of all the other harbors in the whole world. Through these harbors British goods find their way into the markets all over the globe; each one of such harbors constitutes a basis for the conquest of new markets. As far as railroads were of use in assisting British goods to conquer the markets, they were naturally welcomed by Great Britain as instruments of civilisation and progress, and as preparing the way for international fraternity. But whenever it so happened that a railroad did not start from a harbor—that is to say whenever it served to open up directly a Continental market for a Continental State—British indignation knew no bounds; for money was now being earned, and the English had no share in the profits. Thus was England deeply incensed by the construction of the Siberian railroad, and still more so by the prolongation of the latter through Manchuria to Port Arthur. As for the German plan of a Bagdad railroad, i. e. of a line connecting Constantinople (or, if you will, Berlin) with the Persian Gulf, it was in the eyes of the English a direct challenge. It was also an unheard-of insolence, and an "unfriendly act" on the part of the German Government.

The time-honored antagonism of England and Russia in the Near East was bridged over by the Triple Entente. The latter had more than one basis. On the one hand, there was England's hatred, and the coalition which that hatred had forged against Germany; on the other hand, there was Russia's detestation of Austria, and her traditional need of expansion towards Constantinople and the Dardanelles. In addition to these factors there came the doctrine of Panslavism, and this doctrine proved a most useful auxiliary of the above-mentioned "expansive tendencies" of the Russian Government; last but not least came the "guardianship" of all the Balkan peoples, which Russia regarded as a part of her historical mission. British policy had succeeded in checking Russia by means of the Japanese War, and of the conventions concerning Persia and Central Asia; with rare skill had England then managed to concentrate the entire expansive activity of Russia in the Near East. England was here in need of the Russian army. Russia, whom we may well call, as far as Oriental politics are concerned, the hereditary enemy of England, was now employed by the London Cabinet as a battering-ram against Germany and Austria-Hungary.

During many years Russia and Austria-Hungary had maintained a compromise in the Balkans, whereby the solution of the thorny questions at issue was postponed. The same remark applies to the relations between Austria-Hungary and Italy. The latter country's interest in the Balkans had up till now been limited, albeit France, after her reconciliation with Italy, steadily endeavored to distract Italy's attention from Tripoli and Tunis, and to turn it towards Albania. On the other hand, the marriage of the King of Italy with a Montenegrin Princess had *ipso facto* drawn Italy and Russia nearer each other, for the princely House of Montenegro is connected by marriage with the Russian imperial Family. The ancient quarrels between Vienna and Rome, and especially the ever-present hatred of the Irredentists, furnished England likewise with admirable instruments for her "policy of sowing dissension." Finally did Turkey herself become an aim—and an important aim—of Italian policy.

The center-points of the Young Turk movement, of the political importance of which Germany took no notice until a very late period, and which she probably underestimated up till the last minute—the center-points of this movement were in Paris and London. The Young Turks received in these cities their political education, and to a large extent also the resources necessary for their propaganda. The latter had as its object the introduction of more liberal conditions into the Turkish Empire. A *conditio sine qua non* of this introduction was the putting aside of Abdul Hamid. England had always intensely hated Abdul Hamid, especially since he had become a friend of the German Emperor. The London Cabinet was of opinion that the cordial relations between Germany and Turkey were due exclusively to Abdul Hamid, and that the personal friendship between the two Sovereigns had alone rendered possible the railroad and other concessions to Germany. The aim of British policy was, consequently, to get rid of Abdul Hamid as soon as possible. The Balkan Committee and other British emissaries set about stirring up dissatisfaction in the Turkish Empire against him, wherever it was possible to do so; no expenditure was too great for them; it must be admitted that, in such cases, England and her agents are never "stingy" as regards money.

In 1905 Great Britain succeeded, under King Edward's guidance, in obtaining the abrogation of the Mürzsteg Convention which Austria-Hungary and Russia had concluded two years previously. In its place an agreement between the six European Powers was drawn up. England, on this occasion, assumed the leadership; the Island was able to dictate to the Continent in a purely Continental matter. A remarkable phenomenon, and a proof of the ever-growing world-power of England!

England's new policy in the Balkans was labelled "Macedonian Reforms." The London Cabinet took the matter up as accredited spokesman; and France, Russia, and Italy followed in the track of the British Ministers. Since 1903 King Edward went every year to Vienna or Ischl, in order to visit Emperor Francis Joseph, and to develop the "historical friendship" between Austria-Hungary and England. This "historical friendship" had invariably consisted in the fact that Austrian and Hungarian statesmen were weak and shortsighted enough to allow their countries to be misused by England for her own purposes. King Edward's aim, at the time of which we are treating, was to induce Austria-Hungary to let herself be taken in tow by England in the Balkans. If he had succeeded in this, it was inevitable that dissension should break out between Vienna and Berlin. This was what King Edward intended; for in this way, not only would Germany's Oriental policy have been undermined, but the position of the German Empire in Europe would have been weakened. And it should be remembered that Great Britain thus changed her policy in the Near East at the very moment of the European tension due to Morocco, and immediately after the Russo-Japanese War.

In 1908 the Austro-Hungarian Minister for Foreign Affairs, Baron Aehrenthal, published the decision of the Imperial and Royal Government to build a railroad through the Sandjak of Novi-Bazar. The object of this railroad was to establish direct communication between Bosnia and Salonica, and the Treaty of Berlin of 1878 gave Austria-Hungary the right to build it. None the less did the announcement of her intentions create a storm of indignation in Europe. The first peals of thunder came from the direction of Great Britain. It is true that the treaty rights of Austria-Hungary could not be denied either in London or Paris or St. Petersburg; but Austria's action was declared incompatible with the spirit underlying all disinterested international co-operation. The intention was attributed to Austria of utilising her policy of economic expansion towards the Ægean Sea as a sort of "forerunner" for a policy of political expansion, which should bring her eventually to Salonica. In reality the storm in question was directed against Germany rather than against Austria-Hungary. It was hoped to intimidate the latter, and by means of this intimidation to separate her from Germany. The English Press declared that the evident intention was to bring the Balkan Peninsula and the whole of the Near East under Germanic hegemony. The "Servian Question," which was later on to be predominant, appeared on the scene; and under England's leadership, Russia, France, and Italy all supported Servia when she declared that her vital interests would be most seriously endangered by the projected railroad. The Panserb programme included the annexation of the Sandjak of Novi-Bazar by Servia; and the construction of an Austrian railroad through it would have therefore constituted a grave impediment to the realisation of such aims.

The wholly unexpected attitude of England caused profound surprise in Austria-Hungary, who felt herself deeply injured thereby. The fact was that she had never, up till now, realised the real motives of British policy. Austria was proud of her ancient friendly relations with Great Britain; she was conscious of having in former times rendered the latter appreciable services; and, ever since the formation of the anti-German coalition, her statesmen and press had been fond of insisting on the fact that no dissensions existed, or were even conceivable, between the two Powers. Ever since the beginning of the Anglo-German estrangement, the Austro-Hungarian Government had always taken particular care to give repeated public expression to the value which it attached to the maintenance of these friendly relations. Then came also the annual visits of King Edward to Emperor Francis Joseph. In short, Austrian public opinion was sincerely surprised, not to say amazed, when Great Britain, in her virtuous indignation, declared Baron Aehrenthal's railroad scheme to be the greatest infamy of the century. Italy joined the chorus, or rather Great Britain persuaded her to join it. The Italian press never tired of repeating that Italian trade in the Balkans would be seriously damaged after the completion of the Austrian railroad, and that Italy could not permit of Austria-Hungary marching on Salonica. The bitterness created in Italy was one of the valuable successes *d'à côté* achieved by the British campaign.

King Edward and his Ministers continued energetically and perseveringly their propaganda in the Balkans, whereby they defended especially the "Programme of Macedonian Reform." King Edward's celebrated visit to Reval, his meeting with Czar Nicholas, the toasts exchanged, and the semi-official comments in the press (July 19th, 1908), brought the Anglo-Russian negotiations to a conclusion, and constituted so to speak the apogée of the English sovereign's diplomatic triumph. The usual diplomatic assurances to the effect that nothing had been discussed at Reval which was in any way contrary to German interests, could not do away with the impression that King Edward's coalition against the German Empire was now complete. The "Macedonian Question" was considered its best instrument; for the carrying out of the programme of Macedonian Reform would have implied a violation of the Turkish Empire absolutely incompatible with the latter's sovereignty and integrity. The German Empire must, in this way, have been placed before the question as to whether it would abandon Turkey to her fate or not; this question, as the English intended, necessarily led up to the further one: shall we give way or shall we go to war? Austria-Hungary was in the same manner to be placed before a similar dilemma: should she, under such circumstances, still remain by the side of Germany, or should she, in exchange perhaps for compensations, go over to the other side? As we see, quite a lot of prospects and possibilities were opened up to British statesmen; and these possibilities, if cleverly made use of, might lead to the weakening—or, who knows, the destruction—of Germany.

But now something unexpected happened: the Revolution in Turkey. The "Macedonian Reform Scheme" of England, Russia, France, and Italy, had terribly frightened the Turks. Up till now Russia and England had, owing to the divergency of their aims, held each other in check; and it was to this rivalry that Turkey owed the continuation of her existence. The Reval meeting drove home the fact that the two ancient adversaries had come to an understanding in Oriental questions; and this understanding signified the doom of the Turkish Empire. The Young Turks took the European Powers at their word; Abdul Hamid having as yet failed to take "Macedonian Reform" seriously in hand, was deposed; the new rulers drew up a constitution, and inscribed on their banner the maintenance of the territorial integrity of the Empire, and also the equality of all nations and religious bodies therein. In this way was the bottom taken out of the Reval programme. Sir Edward Grey declared himself "satisfied with the turn that matters had taken," and it was decided to give the Young Turks time. England expected the deposition of Abdul Hamid to entail the collapse of the friendship between Germany and Turkey, and at once changed her outward attitude towards the latter. The change, as usual, was very skilfully explained as being a "matter of principle": liberty-loving England, it was said, could not possibly be a friend of the tyrannical and reactionary government of Abdul Hamid; but all the more sincere, therefore, was her joy on witnessing the birth of the new liberal and progressive and humanitarian Ottoman Empire, to which she extended a cordial and hearty welcome. In this way did the British Government think to be able to lift Germany from out of the saddle in Constantinople. It is, unfortunately, not possible to analyse here in detail the policy of England in the Near East since the accession to the throne of Edward VII. But that policy offers, on a small scale, truly typical examples of the skill with which British statesmanship is able to make use even of totally contradictory events in the pursuit of one fundamental aim, which is never lost sight of for a minute. England's calculations after the Young Turk Revolution appeared at first to be successful; and, for a time, she was in fact more popular in Constantinople than Germany. This was only natural, since the Young Turks were continually told that Germany was Abdul Hamid's friend and Young Turkey's enemy—and that she had never really helped Turkey, but had only acted from a purely egotistical standpoint. Only little by little did German diplomacy succeed in again consolidating Germany's position; and some time elapsed before the Young Turk politicians understood that Germany was the only Power whose Oriental policy was compatible with the interests of the Turkish Empire.

In the autumn of 1908 Austria-Hungary saw herself obliged to formally annex the two provinces of Bosnia and Herzegovina, which she had occupied for the past thirty years. It was a necessary step; for the Panserb propaganda threatened to revolutionise Bosnia; and, on the other hand, the Young Turk programme was a national one, and claimed Bosnia and Herzegovina as ancient Turkish provinces inhabited by numerous Mussulmans. Austria-Hungary had either to annex the territories in question, or else to lose them.

This step came as a surprise to England—all the more so, as King Edward had visited Emperor Francis Joseph at Ischl only six weeks before the annexation, and had heard nothing about the proposed measure. The astonishment and fury was so great in London, that even King Edward forgot himself, and dropped his mask. The Austro-Hungarian Ambassador in London, Count Mensdorf, was entrusted with the duty of communicating the annexation to King Edward, together with an autograph letter from his Sovereign. He was received in a most discourteous and unfriendly manner, and himself declared: "I was chased away." As we have already said, the annexation of Bosnia-Herzegovina did not change in any way the existing state of affairs in the Balkans; it only, as it were, put the seal on a document that had been drawn up thirty years previously. None the less did the whole of Europe, at Great Britain's instigation, wax indignant at Austria-Hungary's so-called "breach of faith." In England, and also in France and Russia, the view was expressed that the German Empire was the real moving spirit in the whole business, and that Austria-Hungary had only been led astray. There ensued the celebrated Bosnian crisis, of which, at first sight, Servia appeared to be the center-point. Servia complained loudly about the destruction of her hopes and aspirations, claimed compensations and access to the Adriatic, placed her army on a war footing, and declared *urbi et orbi* that she would not surrender to Austria. In reality, England was the center-point and the *agent provocateur* of the whole Bosnian crisis. The British Government cared nothing for the aspirations of Servia, it cared not about Bosnia, nor about Russia, nor about Italy; it had solely in view the humiliation of Germany and Austria-Hungary, and the destruction of their alliance. It entertained the hope of seeing Germany abandon her ally. Had this happened, it would have been easy to draw Austria-Hungary over to the Triple Entente after the crisis; in this way the whole of Germany's Oriental policy, together with the Bagdad railroad and other concessions, would have come to an end. King Edward expected, therefore, to deal a decisive blow by means of the "Bosnian crisis" which he had organised. The bullet missed its mark, seeing that Germany remained faithful to Austria-Hungary, and adopted the latter's standpoint. Russia and France, on the other hand, were not prepared, in view of the resolute attitude of the Central Powers, to push matters to a head. A skilful diplomatic manœuvre of Prince Bülow made it easier for the Russian Government to accept the annexation of Bosnia-Herzegovina. The crisis was thus brought to an end. Austria-Hungary gained in reality nothing, for she had only preserved herself from otherwise certain injury. Simultaneously with the proclamation of the annexation, the Austro-Hungarian Government gave back the Sandjak of Novi-Bazar to Turkey. But the latter did not, in reality, gain anything by this either. Russia neither gained nor lost anything; and Servia's wishes were not realised. The only country which gained anything was England, for owing to the re-cession of the Sandjak to Turkey, the Austrian railroad plan of which we have already spoken was definitely knocked on the head. The English had no longer to fear the competition of such an international trading route.

England could, in general, be more satisfied with the European situation resulting from the Bosnian crisis, than is generally supposed. Of course, King Edward's plan to destroy the Austro-German alliance, to humiliate these two Powers, and to excite France and Russia against them, had failed. Why? Because neither France nor Russia were ready, seeing that both had been taken by surprise. Neither was England ready. The London Cabinet had reckoned with a slower development of affairs in the Balkans, and it had not foreseen either the Turkish Revolution or the annexation of Bosnia-Herzegovina. Despite their unpreparedness, the British statesmen had put all the wheels of their diplomatic machinery into movement against the German Empire and her ally.

France and Russia had been compelled to admit that they were not ready. This admission, coupled with their diplomatic defeat, was bound to wound both Powers severely in their national pride and in their prestige. This is what Great Britain secretly desired. The British calculation, that henceforth France and Russia would proceed to apply themselves steadily and systematically to the task of developing their military strength, was correct. British policy had also succeeded in making Russia more anxious than ever to rehabilitate herself in the eyes of the Balkan people; it had succeeded in inspiring Servia with the desire of vengeance, not only against Austria-Hungary, but also against Turkey; and the work of exciting Italy against Austria had progressed satisfactorily.

CHAPTER XIV
THE CATASTROPHE IS MORE CAREFULLY PREPARED
1909–1914

The good Germans breathed more freely, and rejoiced at the political *détente*. Their astonishment was all the greater when, at the end of 1908 and the beginning of 1909, a terrible cry arose at the other side of the North Sea about an appalling "German peril." It was stated that the fleet of German Dreadnoughts was in a fair way to out-rivalling that of Great Britain. The cunning tricks of the German Government, and especially of Admiral von Tirpitz, had succeeded in secretly hastening the construction of the German navy. We have already mentioned, in a previous chapter, how skilfully the British Government made use of these lies for the purpose of hoodwinking the Colonies and the United States. The whole story was a falsehood from beginning to end, for there could be no question of the construction of the German fleet being "secretly hastened"; and the British Government knew this perfectly well. The German Government furnished, through its diplomatic representatives and also publicly through the press, more than enough explanations showing that the pretended English reckonings about the number of German battleships were wholly wrong. In the same "year of panic," 1908–09, a conference of the leading maritime nations was held in London, at the invitation of the British Government. The result of this Conference was the publication of the "London Declaration concerning Maritime Law," which was subsequently so much commented upon. Its origin was as follows: During the Conference at The Hague in 1907, the leading maritime nations had declared themselves in agreement with the German proposal to institute a permanent international Court of Prizes. It was intended to convert the latter, in future maritime wars, into a Court of Appeal which should be above all the national Prize Courts. But there was no international law corresponding to the proposed international institution. It was the task of the London Conference to create this international law, and it did so in the form of the London Declaration above mentioned. The avowed object of the latter was to draw up provisions for the protection of neutral shipping in time of war. And, as a matter of fact, the contents of the Declaration were such as to furnish, if not a perfect, at all events a very acceptable basis on which the safety and the rights of neutral shipping could be guaranteed. The British Government instructed its delegates to sign the Declaration, just as in 1907 they had signed the Hague Convention concerning the International Prize Court. But no ratification of either agreement ever took place. The British Government, albeit pretending that it was in favor of the ratification, engineered behind the scenes a violent agitation against the London Declaration, and against the establishment of an International Court of Prizes. This agitation lasted several years. The agitators told the credulous and trembling islanders that the whole thing was just simply a base German intrigue. The German Government had succeeded, according to them, in outwitting harmless British statesmen and naval officers in The Hague and in London. The International Court of Prizes and the London Declaration signified nothing else but "Sea Law made in Germany"; it was intended, in the case of an Anglo-German war, to deprive England of all the means which she possessed for defending her own maritime trade, and to prevent her applying in future those time-honored methods which, in the wars of former centuries, had produced such brilliant results. The British nation was naturally most indignant at this unheard-of German infamy; and the consequence was that the House of Lords, by rejecting a Bill which provided that the existing British Prize Law should be modified, frustrated the ratification of the Hague Convention and also of the London Declaration. When war broke out in 1914 the Declaration did not, therefore, possess international validity; but simple-minded persons in Germany and in the neutral countries firmly believed that England would act according to the provisions of the Declaration, since the latter was the fruit of an unanimous agreement among all the maritime nations which took part in the Conference.

Ever since 1909, it is true, British admirals and statesmen had calmly and coldly proclaimed that it was quite immaterial whether the Declaration were ratified or not, for the moment war broke out "it would be torn into rags and thrown into the sea." The history of the war up to date has proved that the British admirals were well informed. It is true that the rank of an admiral would not have been necessary for that; for it is an old habit of British Governments to announce in the most pathetical tone of voice their readiness to enter into negotiations, and to sign conventions, of this sort. England was always enthusiastic about right and justice in maritime warfare—provided she could by these means bind the hands of other nations without committing herself to anything. We have already shown, in a previous chapter, that England pretended at first to accept the standpoint of the Armed Neutrality League in 1780, and that she afterwards rejected all the desiderata of the League with a sneer. In 1856, in the celebrated Declaration of Paris, Great Britain accepted certain principles to which British naval commanders had not paid the slightest attention during the Crimean War a year or two earlier. The British Admiralty renounced, on the same occasion, its claim to the right of capture—for the times, and the modified conditions of warfare, made it appear unsuitable to raise such a claim. But the Declaration of Paris has never been ratified either, and the British Government did not hesitate for one minute, after war had broken out in 1914, in "tearing it into rags and throwing it into the sea." Notably were the provisions regarding the freedom of cargoes under neutral flag, and those regarding the right of blockade, trampled under foot.

"International Maritime Law": for the pirates who rule the seas, these words have never meant anything else than unlimited freedom for themselves. The English were always glad to see other nations bind themselves hand and foot; with sincere satisfaction did they watch the spectacle of the European nations listening with pious credulity to English speeches about international civilisation and the protection of neutral countries; and when learned professors wrote ponderous volumes on the subject of "the progress and development of maritime law in time of war," the Islanders chuckled with delight. The stupidity of the Continental nations has been as incurable in this case, as in all other cases where the question of the relations between the sacred Island and its European victims has arisen. Great Britain has always been a friend of international parleys, for they have invariably proved a useful instrument for her. At the moment when the Hague Conference of 1907 was being prepared, the British Government endeavored to have a discussion on "the reduction of armaments" inserted in the programme. The object was a double one: firstly, to prevent by means of an international agreement the German fleet from becoming inconveniently strong; secondly, to permit in this way of the British navy maintaining its (at that time crushing) superiority with the least possible expense. King Edward knew that he would have his European coalition unanimously on the side of England. Had the German Government not accepted the decision of the Conference, the German Empire would have been, of course, stamped as the unscrupulous and dangerous disturber of the world's peace. Prince Bülow saw the trap that was being laid, and declared beforehand that Germany would take no part in a debate of this kind. Thus the cunning plan failed, and the British Premier, Sir Henry Campbell-Bannerman, denied indignantly that the London Cabinet had ever intended setting a trap at all. During the following years, British Ministers often attempted to raise the question of a limitation of armaments, and to induce Germany to fall in with their wishes—sometimes by flattery, sometimes by veiled menaces.

The period under review was, in fact, characterised as a whole by England's efforts to check the growth of the German navy by means different to those hitherto adopted. The aim remained the same: namely, to weaken and intimidate Germany. "First humiliate, then destroy": this continued to be the motto. There were many Germans, and amongst them several political men, who did not understand this, who believed in the possibility of Anglo-German friendship, and who understood not the lessons taught by the history of Great Britain. It was about 1909 that the beautiful phrase came into fashion, which we used to hear right up till the outbreak of war: namely, that "Great Britain must and will recognise us as possessing equal rights with herself in Europe and in the whole world." Then, it was declared, the peace of the world would be definitely assured, and the German and the British merchant would work peacefully together; the two nations, related to each other by ties of blood, would henceforth march together along the path of progress towards the conquest of international solidarity. The English even hinted that, in this rosy future, the customs duties would also be suppressed, for they were a hindrance to the intimacy of the two nations. The enormous expenditure on armaments would be reduced to a minimum, and the gigantic sums thus saved would be employed in order to develop the peaceful work of civilisation, instead of being sacrificed to the naval Moloch. He who refused to believe in this message of great joy was denounced, between 1910 and 1914, as a narrow-minded jingo who, in opposition to the will of "the immense majority of the German people," desired to bring about a war between the two "cousins." It was a period which we to-day recall to mind without any pride—a period of self-deception and dangerous illusions on the part of a very large section of the German public. This self-deception was due, in the first place, to the German habit of believing that which it is agreeable to believe; and, in the second place, to a curious misconception concerning the character of the British and the essence of their Empire. When has England, in the whole course of her history, ever recognised a strong and prosperous European maritime nation as possessing equal rights with herself? Never! But, it was argued in Germany, that was in the old times of violence and darkness. Those times were now gone; and England now knew as well as, if not better than, any other nation, that the blessings of peace were much superior even to the advantages reaped from a victorious war. In addition to this, Germany was England's best client, and the British merchant was far too businesslike to wish to lose such a client by weakening or destroying him. Then we must not forget the international ties which bind the modern nations so closely to each other. And finally—*pièce de résistance*—the "common ideals of humanity"! Who could forget them? A few months before war broke out, the German Ambassador in London, Prince Lichnowsky, publicly declared that "nations" and "national ideals" were but stepping-stones leading up to the ultimate ideal of "humanity." So intimately was this diplomatist then convinced of the existence of Anglo-German harmony!

During the last 350 years England has never changed her political and economic aims and methods. Neither the British Empire nor the British nation can be understood unless we know their history. The statesman or diplomatist who does not know or does not understand this history, cannot perceive and cannot understand the unchangeable aim which British policy unswervingly pursues. He must, therefore, infallibly be led astray.

The last alarm was given by the Morocco crisis of 1911. The fundamental reasons underlying this crisis have been, in general, misunderstood in Germany. It is necessary, therefore, that we should briefly dwell on them here. The motive which prompted the German Government to send the

Panther to Agadir was not the inauguration of a new Moroccan policy, but simply the liquidation of the old one. Favored by mistakes previously committed by Germany, French expansion in Morocco could no longer be checked by an appeal to existing treaties; the German Secretary of State for Foreign Affairs, Herr von Kiderlen-Waechter, feared that Germany would one day find herself in a position in which she could no longer claim anything; he therefore decided to have the Panther sent to Agadir in order to compel France to enter into a discussion with the German Government. The latter—we must insist on the fact—intended from the beginning to leave Morocco entirely to France, but desired compensations. As to whether the Agadir demonstration was a well-chosen one, or as to whether the Franco-German negotiations were always conducted as they should have been, this is another question, which we cannot discuss here. However that may be, France proved willing to enter into a discussion; and the negotiations would in all probability have been satisfactorily concluded within a very short time, if England had not suddenly interfered. On the 1st of July, 1911, the Panther appeared in front of Agadir. On July 21st the English Chancellor of the Exchequer, Mr. Lloyd-George, made, after a Cabinet Council had previously been held, a speech at the Mansion House in London. The most important passage of the speech, which was written, was as follows:—

"The potent influence (of England) has many a time been in the past, and may yet be in the future, invaluable to the cause of human liberty. It has more than once in the past redeemed continental nations—who are sometimes too apt to forget that service—from overwhelming disaster and even from national extinction. I would make great sacrifices to preserve peace, I conceive that nothing would justify a disturbance of international goodwill except questions of the gravest national moment. But if a situation were to be forced upon us in which peace would only be preserved by the surrender of the great and beneficent position Britain has won by centuries of heroism and achievement, by allowing Britain to be treated where her interests are vitally affected as if she were of no account in the Cabinet of nations, then I say emphatically that peace at that price would be a humiliation intolerable for a great country like ours to endure."

Four years separate us from the time when these words were spoken, and we can now judge them with impartiality. The speech, made by Mr. Lloyd-George on behalf of his colleagues in the Cabinet, shows us with unusual clearness the British conception of the part played by England in the history of Europe. We have tried, in the course of this book, to give the reader a bird's-eye view of some centuries of that history; England, without one single exception, has been found to be the Vampire of Europe. Her economic policy, her political policy, her wars, have invariably had but a single aim: to drain the riches and the life-blood of the Continental nations. In order to do this, she has systematically stirred them up against each other.—But Mr. Lloyd-George, with true English impertinence, speaks about the "invaluable services" rendered by Great Britain to the cause of Continental freedom; he even dares to talk to Europe about "centuries of heroism and achievement," when the sole object of his country has always been piracy and theft under every conceivable form.

The negotiations between France and Germany in 1911 did not concern England in the least, for they did not touch upon anything belonging to her. Their object was Morocco, which England had long since conceded to France, and also French colonies in Africa. The British statesmen knew perfectly well, however much they may have denied it, that Germany did not intend acquiring anything in Morocco. They knew just as well that Germany only desired to put an end, once and for all, to the friction between herself and France arising from out of the Morocco question. But this was precisely what England could not tolerate. For that reason the passions of the French people were kindled, during the negotiations, by the most idiotic lies manufactured in London. For that reason England interfered with the negotiations, and screamed about the German Empire intending to attack France. All other pretexts and phrases were so many lies, or attempts to conceal the truth. The Moroccan question in itself had only fifth-rate importance for England. But that the two great Continental nations should negotiate together without England, or conclude a treaty without the latter's authorisation: this is what was incompatible with England's century-old traditions. Therefore did British statesmen decide to intervene rapidly and resolutely; and, as is usual in such cases, to utter threats of war. French newspapers in English pay denounced imaginary acts of treason; and the Premier, M. Joseph Caillaux, who was inclined to draw up with Germany an Agreement satisfactory to both parties, was got rid of. The lies spread regarding all sorts of German designs on Morocco and on France, were of English origin. The London Cabinet feared that the great European coalition against Germany might be broken up by a Franco-German understanding. The latter had consequently to be prevented at all costs, and this result was obtained.

The crisis of 1911 showed Great Britain to be the uncontested leader of the anti-German coalition. The London Cabinet would not have been sorry to see war break out at that time, although Russia was not yet ready. The British press, and also the French press which had been corrupted by English gold, loudly demanded war. England finally obtained without war what she wanted: namely, closer co-operation and increased deadly hatred against Germany among the Powers of the Triple Entente.

The military conventions between Great Britain, France, and Belgium, were revised and completed. Amongst other things, the Moroccan crisis had shown that the plan of a British landing *en masse* on the Continent needed to be recast. British experts were of opinion that, during the crisis of 1911, the mobilisation of the fleet destined to transport the expeditionary corps did not work as smoothly as it ought to have done in the case of a war with Germany. The defects were carefully and rapidly repaired, and the machine was kept ready to be put into motion instantly. A definite agreement had been concluded with France, according to which the French fleet was entirely to be concentrated in the Mediterranean, whereas England guaranteed the safety of the Northern coasts of France. Conversations were begun with Russia regarding an active co-operation in the Mediterranean, the Black Sea, and the Baltic. In short, it was clear to the governing circles of England that the next crisis should bring war, or at any rate the complete humiliation of Germany. The three Powers proceeded to develop their armaments on land and sea with the utmost energy.

The controversy concerning the mouth of the Scheldt was characteristic of the situation existing during the years which immediately preceded the war. Holland wished to modernise the forts at Flushing, in order to be able, if need be, to close the mouth of the Scheldt. She had a perfect right to do so; but, at England's instigation, a tremendous hullabaloo was raised in Belgium, France and Russia. The real reason of all the noise was not—as was pretended—that the Scheldt should be kept open for the British fleet, in order that the latter might protect Belgium's neutrality; but it is to be found in the fact that England had already destined Antwerp to be the basis of her operations against Germany in the coming war. The large increase of the Belgian army had been ordered by England, because she desired to see her ally Belgium stronger than had been the case up till then. During many years, the Belgian nation was systematically fanaticised against Germany; and England further induced the Belgian Government to organise a spying service in Western Germany. At the same time, special efforts were again made by the London Cabinet to win over Holland and Denmark for the war of destruction. But such attempts succeeded just as little now as they had formerly done.

The Germans perceived nothing at all of these things. They even believed that the era of intimate and durable friendship with England had dawned. The British Government was very satisfied with this state of public opinion. The War Minister, Haldane, who enjoyed the reputation of being a staunch friend of Germany because he had translated Schopenhauer and took pleasure in making academical speeches about our country, was sent to Berlin early in 1912. The real object of his journey was to endeavor to prevent a further development of the German navy. Haldane himself, backed up by English financiers and the "pro-German" section of the English press, never ceased insisting on the fact that the German navy was the one obstacle in the way of a really intimate friendship between the two countries. The result was, that the German naval programme in 1912 was badly mutilated. On the other hand, England declined the German proposal to conclude a Neutrality Agreement. Haldane returned to London. He could well be pleased with the success of his mission, albeit he had not obtained all he desired. The London Cabinet now knew how strongly the Germans wished to remain on friendly terms with England; above all Haldane brought his colleagues the invaluable information that the British statesmen were, in Germany, considered to be honest. Such wholly unmerited confidence rendered, of course, the work of British diplomacy all the easier. A perfidious diplomacy cannot possibly wish for anything better than to be regarded by its adversary as honest. Every swindler will agree with this.

The Italo-Turkish war broke out; it was followed by the Balkan wars. During the war between Italy and Turkey, England worked hard to detach the former from the Triple Alliance. She did not succeed, because the Rome Cabinet understood that, under the circumstances then existing, it was better for Italy to remain as she was. The same year witnessed the realisation of the important politico-strategical decision of the French Government to concentrate its entire fleet in the Mediterranean. The pretext alleged for the measure was furnished by controversies which arose between France and Italy during the Tripolitan war. France feared—so it was said—the possibility of a closer co-operation of the Powers of the Triple Alliance in the Mediterranean. In this way, popular opinion in Italy was excited against France—but against France only; and the British Government was well pleased at this. The London Cabinet remained, as ever, the good friend and guardian of Italy. But the initial calculation of English and French diplomatists: namely, to separate either Italy or Turkey from Germany, had failed. The campaign in Tripoli, and the seizure of Libya by the Italians, had, on the contrary, drawn Italy nearer to her allies. It is evident that Germany tried as hard as possible to strengthen these tendencies of the Italian Government, and that she made every effort to restore peace as quickly as possible. England, France, and Russia labored just as actively—perhaps even more so—to delay the conclusion of peace.

Under the auspices of Russia, the first Balkan War broke out. The Balkan States had concluded an alliance; they had decided, in agreement with the Russian Government, what was to be taken from Turkey, and how the new territories were to be divided among themselves. Turkey had overestimated her strength; and this mistake had been shared by Germany. After a series of rapid victories, the Balkan States succeeded in conquering nearly the whole of European Turkey. The Bulgarian triumph was even too great for Russia; and energetic pressure from St. Petersburg was necessary in order to stop the Bulgarian advance on Constantinople. This permitted the Turks to gain time, and Bulgaria's strength subsequently proved insufficient. In order to re-settle matters in the Balkan Peninsula, the so-called Ambassadors' Conference met in London, together with the plenipotentiaries of Turkey and the Balkan States. The British Foreign Secretary, Sir Edward Grey, himself presided over the Conference.

The question has been raised in Germany as to whether England knew beforehand that the first Balkan War was going to break out, and as to whether she herself instigated it. It is incontestable that both the British Government and the Balkan Committee knew of the existence of the Balkan Alliance, and were acquainted with the latter's aims. It is, on the other hand, not to be supposed that the British Government directly organised or instigated the war, for the simple reason that it did not need a war. The vehicle put in motion by the British Government was already rolling along the track, without it being necessary to push it; and it is not the custom of British statesmen to give unnecessary publicity to their intentions—on the contrary. The anti-Turkish agitation in the Balkans was always favored by England. As soon as it had been seen that the Young Turks, in spite of their original preference for France and England, had come to recognise that the real interests of Turkey demanded the maintenance of a close and cordial friendship with Germany, the admiration felt in London in 1909 for the new "liberators" came to a speedy end; henceforth no effort was spared by British emissaries to keep up a permanent war in Albania, permanent Armenian unrest in Asia Minor, and a chronic state of revolt in South Arabia: all this, of course, in the name of Christianity, civilisation, and liberty. In 1912 and 1913 Great Britain judged the Balkan problem more or less in the following terms: the destruction of the Turkish Empire in Europe could not be disadvantageous to British interests as such, but it would under all circumstances render the situation of Austria-Hungary and Germany in the Balkans uncommonly difficult, and would necessarily weaken both Powers immensely in the future war. In the eyes of the outside observer British diplomacy had the merit of working for the maintenance of the *status quo*, and in view of the limitation of the war; and this "virtue in the sight of the world" was undoubtedly an advantage. The British Government worked, of course, hand-in-hand with Germany, Austria-Hungary, Russia, and France; it had the greatest admiration for the Balkan States, but also deep sympathy for Turkey, who had, unfortunately, not listened in time to England's disinterested counsels. With laudable energy Sir Edward Grey supported Servia's claims, which were incompatible with Austrian interests; and most intelligently did he encourage Austria-Hungary's policy of temporisation. Devoted, as usual, to the cause of peace, Sir Edward assisted the Powers to create an independent Albania, and then did everything he could to make the Albanian question an apple of discord between Austria and Italy. All these events are too near our own times, and are too directly bound up with the present, for us to be able to submit them here to detailed critical analysis. It is certain that England knew from the beginning that she must inevitably be the winner in the Balkans, in whatever manner the affairs of the Peninsula should develop, and whatever should be the solution of each problem in itself. The secret of England's strength has always resided therein, that she has never allowed her attention to be distracted by secondary problems; she has always had one great main object in view, and she seeks unceasingly to approach ever nearer the realisation of this fundamental aim. She cares not which way is taken, nor what means are adopted, neither does she mind if delays should occur. With the one goal always before her eyes, she works alternately with this and with that Power, appearing first of all as representative of one group of Powers, subsequently as the representative of another, later on co-operating with both, and finally equally far from both; to-day threatening, to-morrow coaxing, the day after to-morrow apparently disinterested and detached, always indifferent to questions of form, and caring only for the substance. Thus it happens that England's political and diplomatic apparatus possesses wonderful freedom of action; that the direction in which the ship of state is steered can be easily changed to suit the winds and the tides; and that the loss of strength due to inner friction is reduced to a minimum.

During the Balkan Wars British policy manifested on more than one occasion friendly and loving anxiety about German interests in the Mediterranean. The London Cabinet took pleasure in tapping the "German cousin" on the shoulder, and pointing towards Syria and Asia Minor—with such insistence that anxiety arose in Paris and St. Petersburg about the "German aspirations." British diplomatists whispered in the ears of the Turks that Germany desired a partition of the Ottoman Empire, and had already prepared for herself a sphere of interest in Asia Minor. In Berlin, on the other hand, the British representatives showed anxious faces; they declared that, as a consequence of the victories of the Balkan States, the position obtained by Russia was becoming a danger for England. It was sought, in this way, to persuade the German statesmen that England needed the help of Germany, and that the former was quite willing secretly to undermine the Triple Entente, and to effect a rapprochement with the German Empire. In reality all these manipulations were the result of careful calculations, and were intended to cast a veil over the real aim of British policy in the Near East. This aim was to accentuate and increase the divergencies between Russia and Germany in that part of the world. Whereas it was endeavored to make German statesmen believe that England was very anxious, and needed Germany's assistance—in other words, that she was being driven by necessity over to Germany's side, the whole thing was nothing but an English trick. As a matter of fact, England had no special reasons for anxiety; for she knew that the further expansion of Russia in the Balkans must call in question the existence of Austria-Hungary; in this way would the great conflict have broken out, or else the Central Powers would have given way. England did not desire a rapprochement with Germany, she only pretended to desire it. The main thing was, that Germany should believe this desire to be sincere. The Cabinets in Paris and St. Petersburg were perfectly at ease about the matter, and knew full well that, should any serious difficulty arise, Great Britain would at once support them actively. Such was the case at the end of 1913, when the question of the German Military Mission to Constantinople arose. When England, this time, took up in conjunction with Russia and France so resolutely hostile an attitude towards Germany, the value of the famous Anglo-German "intimacy" became evident for all those who, having eyes, wished to see things as they were.

He who, in those days, was so foolish as to lack confidence, was always reminded of the Anglo-German negotiations concerning Central Africa and the railroads of Asia Minor. Early in 1914 came the further negotiations concerning petroleum springs in Persia. To-day it is not yet possible to discuss these matters freely and openly, but this much can be said: the Anglo-German negotiations in question were, partly at any rate, means whereby the attention of the Germans might be withdrawn from the systematic and carefully planned development of the preparations for war in England, France, and Russia. In the middle of the Anglo-German honeymoon in 1913 and 1914, British and Russian officers were busy drawing up the Naval Convention which provided for attacking operations to be undertaken in common by the British and Russian fleets in the Baltic, and, in conjunction with the Russian army, against the German coast. The English press spoke a lot about the new friendship with Germany; only when the navies of the two countries came under discussion, did it betray anxiety. Mr. Churchill spoke of the German fleet as a "luxury," and made one tactless attempt after another to bring about a naval "understanding." The object of such an "understanding" was, as usual, to reduce the strength of the German navy in such a way that the British fleet should run no risk in attacking it. Several people in Germany actively seconded these laudable efforts, in order to consolidate the friendship between the two Powers.

About the same time, certain London newspapers, which are known to entertain friendly relations with the British Foreign Office, declared that real peace could not exist in Europe until the "burning question of Alsace-Lorraine had been settled." Once more was the value of the much-vaunted Anglo-German friendship clear to those whose eyes proved capable of seeing things as they were. On either side of the water, enthusiastic speeches celebrated that friendship, while all the time the noise could be heard of the colossal armaments in France and Russia and the language of the French and Russian press was not less menacing than the armaments themselves. In

Germany, all this was declared to be mere boasting. As long as we had England as a friend, everything else was immaterial. The news concerning the immense development of the Russian armaments, and especially the minute care with which they were methodically planned and carried out, was treated in Germany with scepticism. It never occurred to the majority of the Germans that, if England had entertained feelings of sincere friendship for Germany, she would never have tolerated a dangerous growth of French and Russian armaments. The few who insisted on this fact—who maintained that not only did England tolerate the constant increase of dangerous tension, but that she was the leader and organiser of an European coalition against the German Empire: these were treated as "loud-mouthed jingoes" incapable of appreciating the value of Anglo-German friendship.

Let us suppose for a minute that the Heir to the Austro-Hungarian throne had not been murdered in June, 1914; and let us also suppose that the Anglo-German negotiations in the Near East and in Central Africa had been brought to a conclusion, as the Germans had hoped. Would, in this case, a stable order of things have resulted? England certainly hoped for such stability, but only as regards an order of things favorable to her own interests. Her calculation was approximately as follows: owing to the accomplishment of her wishes in Asia Minor and Central Africa, Germany would be kept very busy (in an economic sense) for a long time to come. Much money would be invested in the undertakings, and the tendency to spend immense sums for military purposes would gradually disappear in Germany. The new position of ever-growing importance occupied by Germany in the Near East, would rapidly cause the antagonism between her and Russia to increase. England would often have the opportunity of employing Germany to checkmate Russia, instead of having to intervene directly herself. At the same time, French dissatisfaction with Germany would augment. The German Empire, on the other hand, would have full confidence in England's friendship, and be fully convinced of the latter's pacific intentions. The new colonial undertakings must necessarily multiply the weak spots in the defence of the German Empire, by increasing the number of points where it could be attacked; in this way would the Empire's strength of decision, and its determination to risk everything in a war, be weakened. The German nation would become more and more accessible to the argument according to which Germany, having obtained from England's benevolence all she desired, must in return do her best to show her "good will." The era of "feverish armaments" would be at an end. Viewed from this standpoint, it becomes evident that England's policy of "confidential friendship" aimed first of all at unnerving Germany; after which, a reduction of the latter's military and naval strength must follow as a natural consequence. It would then be all the easier for England's well-armed Continental vassals, France and Russia, either to obtain the break-up of the Austro-German alliance, and the humiliation of the two Central Powers, by threats; or else to force these Powers on to their knees at the point of the bayonet. Whenever necessary, whenever a grave crisis should arise, England would throw the whole weight of her influence into the balance; and her "advice" would be considered the more acceptable, in the measure that the German people were convinced of the sincerity and disinterestedness of British friendship. The only thing necessary was patience.

All these plans were disturbed by the assassination of the Archduke Francis Ferdinand. Events pursued the course that we all know. As soon as the European situation became dangerously strained, the British Government retreated into the background, made perfidious proposals of mediation to Germany, and advised everyone to remain peaceful. We have here, likewise, a time-honored historical method of British diplomacy. In this way does the latter coin the phrases which, once war has broken out, shall serve to justify the British Government, and to inflame the public opinion of as many countries as possible. In this way does that Government collect "unimpeachable" diplomatic documents for Blue Books. In this way does it wait until the final developments of the crisis engineered by England herself produce the great and decisive "phrase," which shall be adopted as the British parole during the war. This time it was the phrase about Belgium's neutrality—a neutrality broken by England systematically for the past nine years. As soon as the great phrase had been coined, England appeared suddenly as the leader of the European anti-German coalition, and proclaimed: Germany must be annihilated, militarily, politically, economically. And, all over the world, deeds immediately followed words. The definitely fixed, carefully planned-out programme had only to be followed. It was followed, and yet are there still to-day people in Germany who maintain that England was led astray by the wicked diplomatists of France and Russia, and was driven against her will into war. Some representatives of this opinion belong to the hopeless category of the believers in an Anglo-German understanding, and even now they blindly refuse to recognise their former errors of judgment; we are not appealing to them. But there are others who have been deceived by the behavior of British diplomacy during the crisis preceding the war. Such behavior is, we repeat, typical. For ten years before the war every single political circle in Great Britain—King, Ministerialists, Opposition—had prepared and organised the European coalition, for the purpose of waging a war of destruction against Germany. The crime of Serayevo brought about the crisis earlier than had been expected. The moment the crisis broke out, the leader of the European coalition retired discreetly into the darkness, made proposals, and preached peace. England maintained that she had not committed herself to either side, that her hands were free, and that she only desired peace. The exchange of diplomatic notes, during the crisis, between London, Paris, and St.

Petersburg, was nothing else but an English *mise en scène*. "Historical documents" they are, but certainly not witnesses to historical truth.

The present war is, as we hope to have shown, a typically English war of destruction waged against a continental rival who was at once envied and feared. The history of the war cannot yet be written in detail. For the purpose of the present book, such a detailed history is not—as we believe to have proved—necessary. But what is necessary is, that the entire German nation should understand where the enemy is and what he wants; it is essential that the German nation should know that this is not an accidental war, but a war carried on with the object of annihilating an economic rival. If England's economic rival is powerless on land and sea, he can be throttled without a war. That was not possible in the case of Germany. British statesmen had always two programmes in readiness, and clearly defined: peace, if Germany gave way and allowed herself to be humiliated; war, if it should be otherwise. Germany desired only peace, believed only in peace, and was convinced that England would take no part in a war against her, if only the German Empire would promise to make no profit out of a Continental war—that is to say, if it would promise to act like a good boy in conformity with what were wrongly supposed to be England's wishes. It was only natural that the London Cabinet should not have accepted this point of view; for it was very far indeed from sharing the German ideas, aspirations, and anxieties! It intended to destroy Germany; and its only concern was: how to arrange the final *mise en scène* which should set the ball rolling.

THE END

Milton Keynes UK
Ingram Content Group UK Ltd.
UKHW030742071024
449371UK00006B/641